7L

Hertfordshire
COUNTY COUNCIL
Community Information

− 3 APR 2001

2 5 JUN 2001

Essex
1|3|02 .

− 8 NOV 2002

2 4 AUG 2005

L32a

10/12

Please renew/return this item by the last date shown.

So that your telephone call is charged at local rate, please call the numbers as set out below:

	From Area codes 01923 or 0208:	From the rest of Herts:
Renewals:	01923 471373	01438 737373
Enquiries:	01923 471333	01438 737333
Minicom:	01923 471599	01438 737599

L32b   748·292'8

THE PEACOCK AND THE LIONS

THE PEACOCK AND THE LIONS

A History and Manual for Collectors of Pressed Glass
of the North-East of England

by

SHEILAGH MURRAY

Sowerby

Davidson

Greener

ORIEL PRESS

STOCKSFIELD

BOSTON   HENLEY   LONDON

Sowerby   Blanc de lait hand-painted bowl

Davidson   Tutankhamun bowl

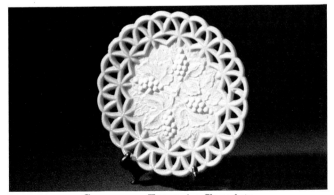

Greener   Turquoise Slag plate

Frontispiece

First published in 1982
by Oriel Press Ltd. (Routledge & Kegan Paul)
Branch End, Stocksfield
Northumberland, NE43 7NA

Set in Mid Century
Printed by R. Gunn & Co. (Printers) Ltd.
Newcastle upon Tyne

ISBN 0 85362 197 7

Photography (colour and black and white)
by J. W. Young, Esq. of the
Department of Photography
University of Newcastle upon Tyne
and
John Williams Photography, Wideopen,
Newcastle upon Tyne

All pieces photographed are in the Author's Collection

Contents

LIST OF FIGURES

List of Plates

SOWERBY GLASS — Coloured Plates continued

SOWERBY GLASS — Black & White Plates

SOWERBY GLASS — Black & White Plates continued

GEORGE DAVIDSON & COMPANY — Coloured Plates (following page 69)

GEORGE DAVIDSON & COMPANY — Black & White Plates

SOWERBY GLASS — Black & White Plates continued

GEORGE DAVIDSON & COMPANY — Coloured Plates (following page 69)

GEORGE DAVIDSON & COMPANY — Black & White Plates

Preface

and

Acknowledgements

The Sowerby, Davidson and Greener firms were the three main glassworks of the North East of England in the late 19th Century. The three symbols, the peacock and the two lions, which were used as trademarks of the firms, are fairly well known, but other details about the factories are very meagre and the glasshouse legends and histories are unrecorded.

I have been fortunate in having as friends Mr. Robert F. Davis, son of Mr. Jack Davis, both Directors of the Suntex Group of Companies, Iver, Bucks. and owners of the previous Sowerby works; the late Mr. Duncan Watson, Manager of Sowerby's Ellison Glassworks from 1957 to 1972, and the late Mr. James Bowran, 90 years old at his death in 1980, for many years the chief mould maker of George Davidson's Glassworks, now Brama Works, Teams, Gateshead on Tyne, and who worked there from 1901 to 1959 when he retired at the age of 71 years.

Through them and the records which were very kindly made available to me by Mr. Robert Davis as well as through innumerable hours of pleasure listening to them 'tell their tales', through visiting glassworks and many contacts and experts, I have collated certain facts and some impressions. These I offer in this volume.

Apart from the above main source information has been gathered from records studied which have included :-

Patent Office - Designs and Trade Marks Act 1881. Registers BT51.

Minutes of Sowerby's Directors' Meetings
    December 1891 to September 1893
    November 1895 to June 1897
    January 1900 to October 1902
    October 1904 to April 1907

Manager's fortnightly Reports 1912 - 1929.

All the above were very legible in the meticulous writing of the time with regular and thick down-strokes of the pen and the flourishes which were typical of the period. The signature of the progressive and artistic Mr. J.G. Sowerby, which was written before 1896, is in interesting contrast (see p.13).

A comprehensive Sowerby scrapbook covering the period February 1912 to July 1929
A Sowerby Account Book (with lock) covering sparsely 1897 - 1906; 1909 and 1910; 1920s.

All these were kindly made available to me by Mr. Robert Davis.

Numerous early Catalogues of Sowerby's Ellison Glassworks.

Davidson's 'Pressed Glass', a booklet by Claude L. Fraser, 1867 to 1948.

Two Davidson Catalogues c.1885, Victoria & Albert Museum, London.

Jobling's publications :- Wear Glass Works, Sunderland.
                            Joblinglass No. 10, March 1969 pp 2 - 7.
                            Glass in the North East, by Nichola Elphinstone

Documents at the Ashridge Repository of the Public Record Office, Berkhamstead, Herts., and from the Public Record Office, now at Kew, Richmond, Surrey.

Current and other literature, see References.

Directories and other documents and maps at the Archives and Local History Department of the Gateshead Public Library, Prince Consort Road, Gateshead.

Day Book, Teams (Flint) Glassworks 1876, Tyne & Wear County Council Archives Department.

Laing Art Gallery, Higham Place, Newcastle upon Tyne, 1.
The Shipley Art Gallery, Prince Consort Road, Gateshead, 8.
The Museum and Art Gallery, Borough Road, Sunderland.
The Library and Museum, Ocean Road, South Shields.
The Beamish Museum, Stanley, Co. Durham.

The firms of W.H. Hepple & Co., of Newcastle upon Tyne, E. Moore & Co., of South Shields and James Hartley and Matthew Turnbull & Co., of Sunderland are briefly mentioned in addition to the three main firms.

I acknowledge the friendly and enthusiastic help of Mrs. Susan Graham with grateful appreciation. She was invaluable in her capacity as my Secretary in Medical and Blood Transfusion work, and she proved equally efficient and expert in her spare time in this province of my hobby.

I have enjoyed and greatly valued the untiring interest and encouragement of my daughter Dinah, whose help has covered every aspect of this project and ensured its completion. She has indeed been my alter ego in this work.

Introduction

I stated in the preface that the symbols of the three main glasshouses in the North East of England were well known, i.e. Sowerby's Peacock and the Davidson and Greener Lions. They have not, however, always been documented with accuracy, the similarity of the lions especially having caused difficulty.

Pressed glass had been introduced in America about 1828 but the first patent for an 'improved glass press' was taken out by Deming Jarves in 1828, and by 1830 mass production of small articles was possible. Many improvements were made over the years, and eventually larger articles such as stemware, lamps, vases, etc., could be pressed.

Sowerby's was one of the first firms to introduce pressed coloured glass into England and certainly bought presses before 1867. They were the leaders in the country and in the forefront in these early days, but fortunes varied and at different periods first one of the three famous firms and then the next was in the ascendancy. There appears to have been rivalry and competition over the years when all three were making fancy goods and coloured art glass, yet there was also a close fraternity encouraged by common membership of the Glass Manufacturers' Association and their common aims - for example, during trade recessions, during their early Union troubles, and during the First World War.

The Peacock head was registered as Sowerby's trademark during the first year in which trademarks were officially registered. The entry below appeared in Volume 23 of Trade & Industry Journal No. 72, May-December 1876.

	JOHN SOWERBY, Ellison Flint Glass Works, Gateshead-on-Tyne; Glass Manufacturer.	15	All Articles of Glass in Opaque Colours.	1285

How the peacock came to be chosen is not known, (See p.15). It will be noted that the peacock is looking to the right and there is no scroll at the base; whereas the peacock impression found on Sowerby articles of the time looks to the left and has an underlining scroll. Occasional pieces of glass can still be found where a full peacock forms part of the decorative pattern, for example the vase shown in Plate 14. It appears to be this peacock head which was used, probably for practical reasons, to stamp the articles.

Davidson's trademark is a demi-lion described either as arising from a turret or a coronet, the latter having three layers with a broken upper fourth layer. A careful search of the Trademarks Register from the first entry in 1876 up to the year 1900 revealed no entry relating to the Davidson firm. By that time the firm had patented their 'Pearline' Series which carry a simple registration number. Although there is no doubt that the lion described was used by the Davidson firm as a trademark, it appears that this was not registered which would explain why no mention of the trademark was made in the small booklet about the firm by Claude L. Fraser. (See Preface). Confusion has often occurred between this lion and the trademark of the Greener firm which is a leaner demi-lion on a torse or torsel, i.e. a single layer scroll.

It is not true that the lions always face a particular way. Difficulty must obviously arise with translucent glass depending upon which way the glass is inspected, but usually, on opaque glass, the Davidson lion does face left. So also does Greener's lion and the differentiation is most easily made by comparing the four-layered coronet of the Davidson lion with the single-layered scroll of the Greener lion. Although Greener's lion is stated in some books to be holding a scabbard, this is not usually so. A few examples can be found where the lion is holding an implement but a scabbard, being the sheath for a sword, is not a proper descriptive term to use. The implement when present is a combined spear and battleaxe and is, therefore, more correctly called a halberd. The Greener trademark has an interesting history and appeared in the official Register as a lion holding a star (see under Greener & Co., p.71)

The peacock's head and the lions may or may not be accompanied by the diamond Design Registration mark from which the date of the design of the article can be accurately deduced. Between 1842 and 1867 for a wide range of goods the letter of the alphabet in the top angle of the diamond indicated the year of design, the sequence being as follows :-

1842	1843	1844	1845	1846	1847	1848	1849	1850	1851	1852	1853	1854
X	H	C	A	I	F	U	S	V	P	D	Y	J

1855	1856	1857	1858	1859	1860	1861	1862	1863	1864	1865	1866	1867
E	L	K	B	M	Z	R	O	G	N	W	Q	T

'V' was recorded as VEE. This is surely as good a random sequence of letters as could have been produced by any modern computer.

A second sequence was used from 1868 to 1883 but now the right hand angle of the diamond contains the year of production letter. As presses were introduced in 1867 by Sowerby's and as this firm was the pioneer of pressed art coloured glass in this country the second sequence is the more important for such glass and the years of production 1868 to 1883 were indicated in the right hand angle as follows:—

1868	X	1874	U	1879	Y
1869	H	1875	S	1880	J
1870	C	1876	V	1881	E
1871	A	1877	P	1882	L
1872	I	1878	W	1883	K
1873	F	(1st-6th March)			
		1878	D		

It will be seen that there was consistency in that the second sequence of letters is the same as the first sequence, apart from a temporary mistake during 1878.

The month of design was shown in the left hand angle in the first period and in the bottom angle in the later period. In both periods the following letter code was used for the month of design:-

January	C	July	I
February	G	August	R (& 1st-19th Sept. 1857).
March	W	September	D
April	H	October	B
May	E	November	K (& Dec. 1860)
June	N	December	A

It is therefore possible to date very accurately pressed glass (Class III) bearing this diamond. Many Sowerby articles carry the diamond registration letters and numbers, as do also quite a proportion of Greener articles. Davidson articles, however, carrying the diamond must be extremely rare if existing at all, which is consistent with the lack of registration of the lion trademark in that period.

Many different designs were often included in one registration. There could, for example, be a basic form with many different decorations and many designs did not specify colour but could be issued in several colours.

From 1884 simple design registration numbers replaced the diamond and these continued in use until 1909. The registered numbers were shown on the articles prefixed by RD and the approximate dates of any article bearing a number can be calculated as follows :-

January 1st 1884 to January 22nd 1885	1	—	20925
January 22nd 1885 to December 21st 1885	20926	—	39953
December 21st 1885 to December 21st 1886	39954	—	63874
December 21st 1886 to January 7th 1888	63875	—	90848
January 7th 1888 to January 15th 1889	90849	—	117439
January 15th 1889 to November 29th 1889	117440	—	139295
November 29th 1889 to February 19th 1890	139296	—	144366
February 19th 1890 to January 27th 1891	144367	—	165353
January 27th 1891 to January 5th 1892	165354	—	185824
January 5th 1892 to December 30th 1892	185825	—	205137
December 30th 1892 to December 28th 1893	205138	—	224604
December 28th 1893 to January 9th 1895	224605	—	247418
January 9th 1895 to February 5th 1896	247419	—	270367
February 5th 1896 to February 8th 1897	270368	—	293588
February 8th 1897 to December 22nd 1897	293589	—	311177
December 22nd 1897 to November 22nd 1898	311178	—	329512
November 22nd 1898 to November 4th 1899	329513	—	348670
November 4th 1899 to December 6th 1900	348671	—	367216

December 6th 1900 to December 12th 1901	367217 —	384526
December 12th 1901 to December 3rd 1902	384527 —	401621
December 3rd 1902 to January 5th 1904	401622 —	424184
January 5th 1904 to January 3rd 1905	424185 —	447602
January 3rd 1905 to January 3rd 1906	447603 —	471608
January 3rd 1906 to February 12th 1907	471609 —	495893
February 12th 1907 to December 7th 1907	495894 —	517231
December 7th 1907 to February 29th 1908	517232 —	520894 *

*This last sequence includes non textile design Nos. 518415 onwards
registered under the Act of 1907

Although following 1867 the three north country firms had concentrated on pressed glass, a few blown and hand decorated articles continued to be made by Sowerby's and are also described in this book. They are particularly desirable and a pleasure to acquire. (See Plate 34 showing two articles in the Venetian Series).

Chapter I

Sowerby Glass

SOWERBY GLASS (i)

The Sowerby name and its trademark of a peacock's head are fairly well known, but only as indicating pressed 'slag' glass of the late 19th Century in the North East of England. There are many gaps to fill in, for it is seldom appreciated that this firm, which when started was entitled the New Stourbridge Glass Works, had connections going back to the start of the Century and even earlier. The firm has left an interesting legacy of glass for the collector.

On August 12th 1809, a notice appeared in the Newcastle Courant from the New Stourbridge Glass Works, Gateshead, stating that the business 'heretofore carried on under the firm of Robertson Seager and Co. was this day dissolved as far as regards James Seager and will in future be carried on under the firm of Robertson & Co.'

Two years later in 1811 Richard Sowerby, a glass manufacturer and a partner in the firm of Robertson & Co. died. It is not known how long he had been a partner but it is clear from the records that the New Stourbridge Glass works was already in existence at the side of the river Tyne in Pipewellgate at least at the beginning of the 19th Century. A district descriptively called Rabbit Banks in Pipewellgate was made up of New Chatham and the adjacent New Stourbridge and this location containing many glassworks accounts for the original name of the works, which eventually became the Sowerby Glass Works.

On 1st February, 1812, a Notice was published that the partnership 'lately carried on by John Robertson, Joseph Miller, Thomas Thompson, Richard Sowerby (deceased), Hindmarsh Thompson and William Birkinshaw under the firm of John Robertson & Co. as Flint Glass manufacturers at New Stourbridge near Newcastle upon Tyne was amicably dissolved on 31st December last and the same concern will in future be carried on by John Robertson, Robert Hood, George Sowerby and William Birkinshaw under the firm of John Robertson & Co., who received all debts due and would pay all debts owing from the late Partnership.' Mr. William Birkinshaw was thanked for friendly aid in writing an article about the glass industry in 'The History of Northumberland' [1] in 1811. In this History a visiting Frenchman recorded that 'All the glass manufacturers in Newcastle 'though established in buildings of a mean appearance are managed with a simplicity and economy which cannot be too much praised. This modest simplicity is of great advantage to the country. It encourages active and industrious men to embark in trade, who would otherwise be unwilling to form large establishments being alarmed by the expenses ..... It is a taste for pomp and grandeur which almost always ruins the manufactories of France.'

From 1812 George Sowerby was shown in the local Directory [2] as of New Stourbridge with his residence at Shipcote, Gateshead. He was also listed as a coal owner. He continued in the glass partnership which soon became Robertson, Hood, Sowerby and Birkinshaw and in 1816 it became the firm of Sowerby and Lowry.

Around 1824, George Sowerby became the owner of the New Stourbridge works and must have flourished because in the 13th Report of the Commissioners of Excise Inquiry he was shown paying, as a glassmaker, a duty of £6,705.19.6d for the year 1833 [3]. He was a man of substance and of considerable activity in public affairs, being a Church Warden in 1828, on the Town Council in 1835, and Mayor of the Borough in 1842.

It appears that his son John Sowerby followed him in 1838 as the flint glass manufacturer at New Stourbridge, Pipewellgate, and he also lived at Shipcote, Gateshead. See Fig. 1 (Billhead of New Stourbridge Glass Works).

In 1850 the Sowerby firm turned to the Midlands for labour and thirty families came to Gateshead in a special train chartered from Birmingham - George Stephenson's railways were in their infancy and a 'Puffing Billy' with open carriages, going at twenty miles per hour transported the work force. The works then were by the riverside, and the families settled in the Chandless Street area and formed a little colony. At the turn

Fig. 1   BILLHEAD OF NEW STOURBRIDGE GLASS WORKS.

of the century there was much roisterous living in Public Houses, and shops stayed open till midnight - so stated a Mrs. Brown at the age of 78 years in 1962 according to a cutting from the Newcastle Evening Chronicle. In 1898 at the age of 14 years Mrs. Brown had worked in the large house of the Sowerby family in Mulgrave Terrace, Gateshead. For 2/6d. a week she worked long hours 'in service', and later earned her living at the Glass-works. Other Sowerbys were in the trade for she mentions Joseph Sowerby's two sons, William and Thomas, who were both expert engravers. Her report has atmosphere for she continues, 'As for characters! the one all the older people seem to remember best is Tommy on the Bridge, who used to get drunk and then stand on the Swing Bridge with one foot in Newcastle and one in Gateshead and daring the police from either side to arrest him. 'Sawdust Jack' used to drive his horse and cart around selling fresh sawdust to keep the floors of shops and pubs clean and sweet smelling.' The same report states that 'In the 19th Century Gateshead had become a busy town. For a long time the main railway line from London stopped at Gateshead and passengers for Newcastle had to leave the train and cross the river themselves. This gave Gateshead a feeling of superiority, but the railway bridges were built and gradually Newcastle became dominant again.' In fact Gateshead remained the terminus for only a short period of five years, the first railway bridge was built in 1849 [4].

A Sowerby scrapbook quotes an old record of September 23rd, 1823 — 'The workmen employed in several of the glasshouses in Newcastle and Gateshead made a procession through the principal streets of the town, each bearing in his hand a specimen of the art, remarkable for its curious construction or its beauty and elegance.'

'The morning was ushered in with the ringing of bells and notice of the intended procession having been given, numbers of persons crowded the streets. A little after twelve o'clock it moved forward along the Close amid cheers of the assembled multitude and the firing of cannons and preceded by the band of the Tyne Hussars.'

'The hat of almost every person in the procession was decorated with a glass feather, whilst a glass star sparkled on the breast, and a chain and collar of variegated glass hung round the neck.'

'A glass bugle which sounded the halts and played several marches was much admired. When the procession arrived at the Mansion House it halted while a salute was fired from a fort mounted with glass cannon to the astonishment of spectators.'

It is certain that the New Stourbridge glassworkers took part in such galas and grand doings. 'The Stourbridge', Gateshead was mentioned in the 'Local Records' by Sykes [5] as among the works represented which were preceded by the band of the Tyne Hussars. This also records that 'Each man carried a staff with a cross piece on top displaying one or more specimens of the glassmaking art, such as decanters, goblets, jugs, bowls, glasses,' and it mentions that there were two elegant glass bird-cages, containing live birds, which sung at periods during the procession. A 1907 report [6] describes how the men of each works used to march in seniority order and were identified by coloured sashes - the Gateshead workers wearing blue silk sashes trimmed with orange.

In 1854 there was a disastrous fire [7] which started in a worsted factory on Gateshead Quayside and spread to an adjoining chemical warehouse. Newcastle and Gateshead for once united in the face of possible disaster. According to an Evening Chronicle report of 1962 about Gateshead in the previous Century, 'Fifty soldiers with fire fighting equipment were sent over the river from Newcastle to help. But they were too late. As they approached the burning buildings came the famous explosion. Its noise and violence resembled the eruption of a volcano . . . . . Flaming debris was thrown hundreds of yards to crash on top of the watching crowds on the Newcastle side of the river to start the biggest blaze the city has ever known. Special trains ran every hour in the succeeding days to cope with the crowds who would see the scene of destruction.'

A contemporary account written in 1854 so that profits could go to the relief of sufferers records that 'workmen in Monkwearmouth Colliery, the deepest in the Kingdom and at least 11 miles from Newcastle heard the explosion and hurried out in alarm.' [8] This factual account indicates how the Gateshead inquest and enquiry was adjourned many times because of charges and investigations about the possibility of stored gunpowder having caused the explosion. John Sowerby, as the Foreman, and Samuel Neville were on the jury of this inquest whose verdict was that gunpowder was not responsible, but that the accidental explosion had occurred by nitrate of soda and sulphur reacting chemically or mechanically. They recommended that these substances should not be stored or deposited near to each other.

In the year 1856 John Sowerby is still shown in the local Directory as at the New Stourbridge Glass Works by the river, while Samuel Neville is shown as a glass manufacturer of Ellison Glass Works at East Street, Gateshead. The Nevilles were an old influential family who were Lords of Northumberland and Westmorland and their town residence in Newcastle gave the name to Neville Street. Samuel Neville who made his home in Gateshead belonged to a remote branch of this distinguished family. John Sowerby married Samuel Neville's daughter and the two men formed the firm of Sowerby and Neville (Flint) Ellison Glass Works in 1857. I.W.S. of Barking in Essex at the age of 77 years (born 1843) wrote, 'I watched the first part of the erection of the Ellison Glass Works in 1852. The firm by 1857 had changed into Sowerby and Neville.' The partnership Sowerby and Neville, operating from the Ellison Glass Works, continued until about 1865. A price list with the heading Sowerby and Neville, dated 1st May 1861 has been inspected and included 12" centre dishes and stands at 6s.0d., Caroffs (carafes), Ales, Cans, Celeries and Decanters, and an account similarly headed for £5.5.4d. to a Mr. Fox of Bradford was dated 10th October 1865. The Writer has seen also an impressive parchment - the Indentures of Henry Brown 'in the 29th year of the Reign of our Sovereign Lady Victoria, 1865', signed on behalf of Sowerby and Neville. At this time the firm was renowned.

It is perhaps understandable how confusion has existed and how both George and John Sowerby have each been called the firm's founder. John was certainly the first Sowerby in the Ellison Works but George Sowerby had owned the New Stourbridge Glass Works many years before and Richard and perhaps other Sowerbys were concerned in partnership at the New Stourbridge Works even earlier. This perhaps accounts for statements about the firm producing hand made table glass in 1765, but there is only flimsy evidence from 1940 [9] for this dating when an employee of Sowerby's stated that the firm had existed for over 175 years. Apart from the above facts few details are known of those early days but it does seem that the Sowerby family and their products must have contributed to the high reputation of Newcastle as a glass centre.

Early Historical Note about Newcastle upon Tyne [10, 11]

Because of the loss of timber from the countryside due to glassmaking and the resultant national resentment, the use of wood as a fuel for this trade was prohibited in 1615. In 1613, Sir Robert Mansell, Vice Admiral of England [12] had established a glass factory in Lambeth using Scottish coal instead of wood, but when wood was prohibited as a fuel he looked for other districts with coal and with easy waterway transport facilities, i.e. a navigable river the banks of which were suitable for building. His first glassworks on Tyneside were established in 1619, and by 1624 Mansell produced up to 8,000 cwts. of finished glassware per year from three glasshouses on the original Newcastle site. At this time he had the sole right to carry on the glass industry in England and this position obtained for twenty years when the Civil War (1642-1646) ended his monopoly. To King James it was a wonder, 'that Robin Mansell being a sea-man, whereby he got so much honour, should fall from water to tamper with fire, which was two contrary elements.' [12]

In 1684 some members of the Italian Dagnia family, who had been producing glass in Bristol, established glasshouses in the West of Newcastle and were the first to produce flint glass.

Earlier, perhaps as early as 1670, the French Huguenot families of Henzell and Tyzack worked glasshouses to the East of the City of Newcastle and by 1736 there were seven glasshouses on the East side, all except one being worked by the Henzell and Tyzack families specialising in window or 'broad' glass and, later in glass bottles.

The influence of these families began to wane in the latter part of the 18th Century and it ceased after the death in 1769 at the age of 82 years of the able glassmaker Mr. Joshua Henzell who was 'esteemed the most corpulent person in this part of the country.' His descendants had not been so financially successful and the glassworks were sold to Matthew Ridley and later were controlled by Sir Matthew White Ridley from 1765. At the end of the Civil War (1646) and continuing for almost two centuries there was a tax on glassmaking which, because oppressive, probably contributed to the development of the famous Newcastle light baluster glasses which were produced from 1730 until 1780. This was the time (from 1763 to 1778) when William and Mary Beilby were undertaking their superb enamelled decoration of drinking glasses, goblets and bowls [13, 14] , and when so many Newcastle glasses were sent to Holland for diamond point engraving.

The Sowerby connections through the New Stourbridge Works stretch back almost to this famous and distinguished time. In the year 1811 more glass was manufactured on the River Tyne than in all the vast Empire of France. [1]

SOWERBY'S ELLISON GLASS WORKS LIMITED

Samuel Neville, having entered into partnership in 1857 with John Sowerby at the Ellison Works, left East Street in 1865 and built a new glassworks on a site close to the present Newcastle Central Station in what is still called Neville Street, but this venture lasted only a short time and he retired in 1872. The firm he left in East Street became Sowerby & Co., and continued in the Ellison Works, but these changes must have caused considerable trade confusion for although the Sowerby catalogue (Pattern Book IX) of June 1881 is entitled Sowerby Ellison Glass Works and the previous No. VIII was entitled Sowerby and Co., later pattern books of 1895 and even up to 1907 (No. XIX) still carried the legend 'Sowerby and Neville and Sowerby and Co. merged into Sowerby's Ellison Glass works Ltd.', and a footnote explained that as a Lincolnshire firm was already registered as Sowerby and Co. Ltd., the different title for the limited company had necessarily been agreed.

From 1857, John Sowerby always attended the Ellison Works in East Street dressed in a frock coat and silk hat and these garments were preserved and displayed at the Ellison Works until 1948. He lived at Benwell Towers, a handsome property (see Fig. 2) designed by the architect John Dobson in 1831, which later became the residence of the Bishop of Newcastle. It shows an example of the architect's particular flair for corner design. [15] John Sowerby died at Benwell Towers on 19th March 1879.

BENWELL TOWERS

Fig. 2   Sketch of Benwell Towers

J. G. SOWERBY, Artist & Glassman

* Facsimile signature

J. G. Sowerby

John Sowerby's son, J.G. Sowerby took his father's place in the company and he appears as a more colourful man - perhaps because more details are known. He was an expert oarsman, and it is on record that he won a skiff race from the Mansion House to Scotswood Suspension Bridge by nearly one-third of a mile, receiving a valuable piece of silver plate as prize. He was fond of the gun and dogs, and was interested in promoting boat racing, boxing and wrestling amongst his workmen. Indeed he had a room specially built at the Works to train the men in these sports. He held sports gatherings at his home, Benwell Towers, and was also responsible for the formation of a band amongst his workmen. The band did not endure long, however, because it disappointed him and there was no resumption of activities after a trip to Rothbury in mid-Northumberland which, being over-enthusiastically enjoyed by the band resulted in many of the instruments being found scattered and abandoned in various parts of Newcastle the following morning.

J.G. Sowerby was a talented landscape artist, who had thirteen pictures hung at the Royal Academy and nine works hung in other London Exhibitions [16]. After his retirement to the country at Chollerton, Northumberland and a subsequent move to the South of England he wrote a book entitled 'Rooks and their Neighbours'. [17] This extraordinary book, published in 1895, sets out to be not a thesis or research document, and not a popular natural history 'merely some desultory gossip about Rooks and their Neighbours'. In fact, it allows an insight into the author and his lifestyle. He sketched and painted the 38 watercolours used as illustrations for the book. The text shows him as a family man, interested in his children but above all a lover of nature and a persistent recorder over many years of the habits of rooks. He remembers even as a youngster the 'exciting hours' spent with a farmer's boy in a hedge adjoining a cornfield waiting for the coming of the 'black robbers'. We learn that he had a son at Winchester and that he rented an old-fashioned house in Surrey. He also made reference to the childrens' nurses, and to their pets - cats, kittens, a fox terrier puppy called Boots, etc. He talks of African marigolds, flowerbeds and a trout stream 20 feet from the house. He was very fond of the month of December. The initial letters of many of the chapters in his book have his own illustrations as part of the capital letters (Fig. 3) and it can be seen how these are analagous to his illustrations of other books and to those which his daughter Millicent produced for other publications. It has been pointed out[18] how J.G. Sowerby's illustrations showed the marked influence of Kate Greenaway. Another of his daughters, Kate Githa Sowerby, later became a well-known playwright. (See p.52).

---

* Signature on inside cover of J.G. Sowerby's personal copy of a book, Glass in the Old World by M.A. Wallace-Dunlop (1883). Field and Tuer, London, E.C. Remarkably different to the common calligraphic style of the period.

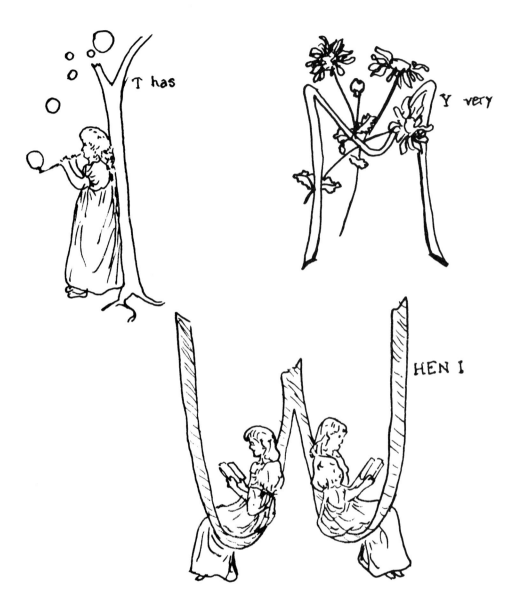

Fig. 3   Examples of initial letters of chapters in J.G. Sowerby's book
'Rooks and their Neighbours'

J.G. Sowerby was an able glass man, imaginative and progressive even by modern standards, who presided over the firm at its peak. In 1883 sales for one month amounted to £4,471 which was a record not surpassed for the following 31 years until 1914. Trading in many countries, and with artistic interest and ability, it is not hard to understand why at that time he would choose a peacock as a trademark for this bird was becoming a universal symbol· of Early Art Nouveau in many crafts. [19,20]

The trademark was registered in January 1876, i.e. in the year when Trademarks were first introduced.[21]

J.G. Sowerby has not yet been given his proper place among artists of this period and many museums at present lack proper coverage of the best examples of his glass designs and colours (see later p.16 et seq).

SOWERBY GLASS (ii)

SOWERBY COLOURS AND PATTERNS

Many colours were introduced in manufacturing by J.G. Sowerby and he gave much time to the Company as Director Manager. The Sowerby 'Common' colours as advertised in their catalogues of that time were Green, Puce and Blue which were offered at the same price as similar Flint articles. So-called 'best' colours of Canary and Pomona (a green in which yellow predominates) had 50% added to flint prices and all other goods had 33⅓% added to flint prices. 'Best' colours were kept in stock and could be ordered in any quantity but other coloured goods had to be ordered in quantities of not less that fifty shillings in value for each article in each colour.

His cousin George Sowerby visited America on behalf of the firm in 1880 with as many as 2,000 samples for display. The American 'Pottery and Glassware' reporter is quoted [22] as stating that although George Sowerby was quite a young man he was 'thoroughly posted in all that appertains to the glass trade'. George Sowerby left the Ellison Works and took ownership, with his sons, of the Northumberland Glasshouse at Lemington in 1898. This project lasted only 8 years, but at the works, now in the hands of Glass Bulbs Limited, the old 'high cone' still stands. It is 130 feet high and was said to have been the largest cone ever erected over a glass furnace and to have had 1,800,000 bricks used in its construction. [11]

Book VIII.

Pattern Book VIII of Sowerby & Co., dated approximately 1880, proclaimed Sowerby's Ellison Vitro-Porcelain wares which were available in Turquoise, Gold, Jet and Opal - the latter colour being the most common at the time, and probably accounting

for more than 50% of the output. These Vitro-Porcelain wares are generally known now as slag glass although the Opal remains separate.

Various 'malachite' Vitro-Porcelain colours were also described - the malachite wares have a 'marbled' effect and are to be found rarely in green, blue and brown malachite in that order. The more common purple malachite, now colloquially called blackberries and cream slag by some dealers, was made a year or so later. Typical pieces are shown in Plates 1. and 2. Although Sowerby's

produced the greatest quantity of purple slag glass it was produced also by the other main N.E. firms. Without the trademarks or the identification of known patterns it is often difficult to distinguish the products of the different firms. Plate 3 shows for comparison a small ornament in purple slag glass in the shape of a crinolined lady. This is not marked but is probably American. Plate 4 shows a Sowerby very good quality purple malachite basin on a stemmed foot which has a blue colour introduced with the purple and white. Purple malachite is available fairly frequently and often is of very good quality. Plate 5 shows a green marble salt with the Sowerby mark. Both green and blue colours are rare but the rarest is a light brown malachite 'marble' glass.

JET GLASS

The name slag glass was first given to jet glassware which undoubtedly contained 'slag' or dross from coal or iron works in the neighbourhood. The term slag now includes all the opaque coloured ware of that time whether or not iron or coal siftings, slag or dust was used. In fact slag has become synonymous with the opaque Vitro-porcelain wares as described at the time, excluding opal glass.

1160

The jet example of 1880 in Plate 6 with a remarkably clear peacock is expertly manufactured and has a better flint glass as a basis than the later jet goods. The brilliancy of this article indicates the addition of coal dust in the recipe instead of only ground coke. (See p.33).

A basin of cauldron shape with matching jug is shown in Plate 7 and is probably not a Sowerby pattern. This pattern is fairly frequently seen. Most of these articles are unmarked but the basin in Plate 7 has a thistle trademark on the inside and it is probably of scottish origin.

Pattern No. 1160 is a fairly common Sowerby pattern to be found in Jet glass. These also are usually unmarked unless made in another colour, for example, pale blue slag.

17

OPAL GLASS

Rare examples of the early Sowerby Opal glass are shown in Plates 8 & 9. This first rather faint-coloured Opal glass was probably manufactured in 1877 — one article shown (Plate 8) produced in April 1879, is a small square vase and depicts classical figures on each of its four panels. The other article is a double salt dated c 1880.

A translucent glass of the same texture and formula as Sowerby's Opal glass but with a lovely deep pink colouration is extremely rare and dates from the same time.

Gladstone Bag Pattern

I have seen two examples of a Gladstone bag ornament in this colour which can be dated 1877 from the diamond Registration mark. They were part of Ursula Lady Ridley's collection now held by the Shipley Art Gallery in Gateshead.

The Sowerby faint-coloured opal gave way to a stronger looking opal 'mix' some time later as in the 'Swan Vase' dated August 1879 shown in Plate 10. It has a stronger bluish tint and is more ochre in transmitted light. This is the same type of glass used later by Lalique and often attributed to him, but it was not until twenty years later, i.e. after 1900 that Lalique started his early experiments and concentrated on production of glass. [23] An idioartistic opalescent glass dish of about 1924 depicting Mermaids bathing in spray and entitled 'Sirens' is marked 'R. Lalique France No. 3003' and is shown for colour comparison alongside the much earlier Sowerby swan vase. (Plate 11).

The first production of coloured glass in the mass by the famous Emile Gallé, which he entitled Clair-de-lune glass, is more interesting in this context. It has been described as of opalescent tint, showing a sapphire blue colour in certain lights [24]. and Gallé first exhibited it in 1878. It is stated that rival manufacturers imitated the effect which in England they called Moonlight glass but the small pressed 'Opal' vase described above is evidence of probably at least concurrent if not earlier production by Sowerby's of this colour. It is certain that J.G. Sowerby had shown great interest in colour and much development work had been undertaken by him.

SELECTIONS OF SOWERBY PATTERNS
from BOOK VIII and JUNE 1882 BOOK IX

Selections of Sowerby Patterns from Book VIII and Book IX continued

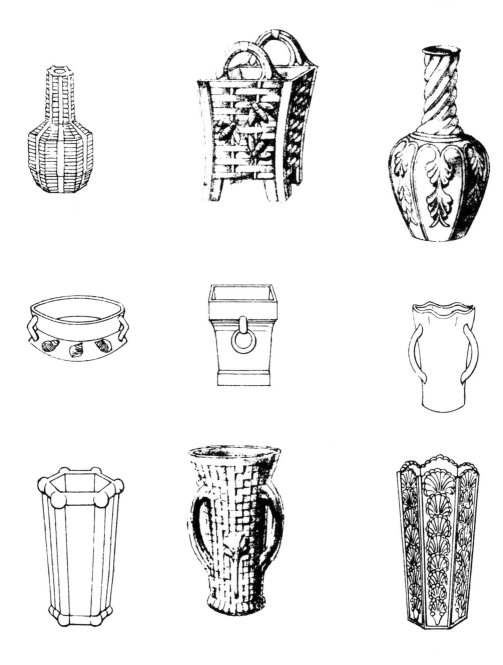

Selections of Sowerby Patterns from Book VIII and Book IX continued

1061

GATESHEAD STAINED GLASS CO. LTD.

J.G. Sowerby had researched for some years into ways of producing stained glass windows, and having introduced coloured glass successfully into the Sowerby firm for domestic articles he formed the Gateshead Stained Glass Company Limited in 1885. This important business had been inaugurated earlier as a department of Messrs. Sowerby's Glassworks and its general manager was H.C. Drummond. A report on Tyneside in 1889 [25] stated, 'One of J.G. Sowerby's specialities was a form of antique glass having a wonderfully soft yet brilliant effect, by means of which he was enabled to show the veining of flowers and the folds of drapery in the glass itself without the aid of the more or less opaque enamels in ordinary use'. A great deal of very beautiful work in this patent glass was carried out by Mr. Sowerby. The department was formed into a Limited Company in 1887 but a unique feature was that the principal employees were shareholders, and were financially supplemented by outside capitalists. It was the largest undertaking of its kind in the North of England and it prospered. The Company 'furnished, free of charge, estimates and designs for every description of ecclesiastic and memorial windows, plain and ornamental leaded glazing, art tiles and general glass decoration for churches, public buildings, hotels, ships, private residences, etc., all executed in the best modern style by skilled workmen who use only the finest materials'. Their contracts included the New Law Courts in London, the Marquis of Bute's mansion at Rothesay, important work in Manchester, St. George's Church in Jesmond, Newcastle and many assignments abroad. 'Their high artistic standard was unfailingly maintained in each and every undertaking'.

SOWERBY NUGGET WARE AND PELOTON GLASS

Some of the vases described in Catalogues VIII and IX already mentioned were made in blue and black using small pieces of silver or gold paper in their manufacture, the wares being called 'Nugget ware'. Examples can be seen in the Laing Art Gallery, Newcastle upon Tyne, along with other desirable wares of that time which were cased or decorated small vases. A small vase with black casing and a deep blue interior is held by the Shipley Art Gallery, Gateshead. The decorated vase in Plate 12 shows opaque white glass filaments which have been fired into a green glass (Pattern No. 1244, Book VIII 1880). This is somewhat akin to Peloton ware, described as applied vermiculated decoration by A.C. Revi [26] who stated that in 1880 J.G. Sowerby of Gateshead on Tyne, who had been fascinated at the time with possibilities for production of stained glass windows, 'registered a patent for producing sheets of glass with threads of coloured glass scattered over its surface'. This patent was in advance of Bohemian William Kralik's patent named Peloton glass and before the formation of the Stained Glass Company in Gateshead dealing with window glass in 1885. Two small blown flint vases with white Peloton decoration shown in Plate 13 have a Sowerby appearance and perhaps were the fore-runner of the better known 'fired' white decorated Sowerby pressed vases mentioned above. An ability to recognise the differences in examples of glass from different firms comes from experience using pattern, aura, techniques, colour and style in assessment.

Pattern Book

JUNE 1882. BOOK IX

*Opal, Turquoise, Gold, Jet, Venetian in several colours.
Giallo, Blanc-de-lait, Malachite.*

Patent Ivory Queens Ware.

DECORATED·OPAQUE·STAINED·BLANC·DE·LAIT.

and new

TORTOISE·SHELL·WARE.

Pattern Book IX of Fancy Goods manufactured by Sowerby's Ellison Glass Works Limited carried the above legend on the outside cover and was dated June 1882. It described Flint, Opal, Turquoise, Malachite, Patent Ivory Queen's Ware, Blanc de Lait and new Tortoiseshell ware. The last named is extremely scarce.

The list of offices advertised on the front of the catalogue included Gateshead, London, Birmingham, Paris and Hamburg, and the catalogue contained drawings of numerous designs of vases, spills and baskets. A peacock vase and a Font vase in Queen's ware and blue slag respectively are shown in Plate 14.

Adventurous patterns were produced, such as attractive swan vases - for this bird had joined the peacock as an Art Nouveau symbol. Examples (Plate 15) are shown in Queen's ware and an unusual lime green. The same article was made in a darker green and in a strong yellow colour.

I have seen it also in black where the reeds and water in the pattern were shiny but the swans had been acid treated giving a matt effect.

BASKET WEAVE PATTERNS

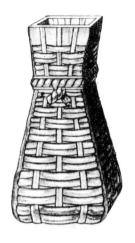

The basket weave pattern for vases, spills, plates and dishes (Plate 16) was very successful, hard wearing and popular, and quite a number of examples have remained intact to the present day, especially the plates. Most of them carry the peacock mark. Two varieties of plate were produced - one larger and deeper which was sold with a separate three-footed stand (Plate 17), the other was a shallower plate without a stand. Plates were made in various colours but pale blue slag and white are the colours often found nowadays and only occasionally are black, coloured malachite, olive green, or iridescent examples available.

Two or three years ago when staying in a hotel in Crieff, Scotland, I was intrigued to see bread rolls for dinner being offered in a blue slag weave-pattern deep Sowerby dish which was in everyday use, and had been for countless years. Its age was not appreciated and even though no special care was being taken there was not a chip or a crack in the article.

Plate 18 shows a white ribbon plate. This is also basket weave pattern but has a border through which a ribbon can be slotted to decorate and display the plate if desired.

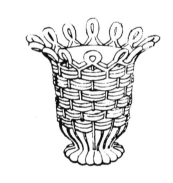

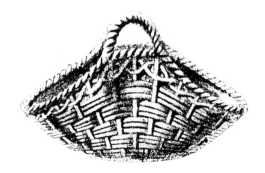

SELECTIONS FROM JUNE 1882, BOOK IX

Selections from June 1882, Book IX continued

CRYSTAL TABLE GLASSWARE from BOOK XI
and CONTINUATION of BOOK XI

May 1st 1885

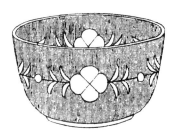

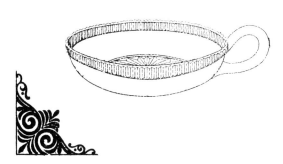

D

RHYME AND NURSERY THEMES

Nursery rhyme themes for decoration were popular depicting for example, Oranges and

Lemons, Mary Mary Quite Contrary, Little Boy Blue, Jack and Jill, Jack Horner, Old King Cole, Little Bo Peep, etc. They are frequently found in pale blue, true white, and in Queen's Ware (see later). They necessitated careful design and expert production of the moulds and they were popular over a number

of years. Plates 19 and 20 show typical articles, themes, shapes and colours.

The purple malachite vase shown in Plate 20 with Spinning Wheel pattern is unusual. Such nursery rhyme articles are rare in this type of glass, the nature of which obscured the pattern.

HAND-PAINTED PRESSED GLASS

Hand-painted pressed articles are unusual. An exceptional example, a Sowerby white slag beaker, has been described and illustrated in colour [27]. The moulding shows school boys at a bench and the clothes of the boys are painted in rust and green, and the hair in ochre colour. Other hand-painted examples have been illustrated [28,29] but they are extremely rare.

A hand-painted small bowl in white with brick colour and green painting of the flowers and leaves is shown in Plate 21 along with another white bowl on four small feet with paler colouring. See also Frontispiece. I have recently found a matching small cream jug which makes a nice set. A small vase with the flowers outlined in gilt is also shown.

An early rare Opal bowl hand-painted in ochre is shown in Plate 22.

PATENT QUEEN'S WARE

Queen's ware was a creamy coloured slag glass and Sowerby's best designs were used for this type of ware with some extremely intricate moulds and it was always the most highly priced. Usually pieces of Queen's Ware are to a high manufacturing standard and seldom is a shoddy example seen. Most of these pieces are marked and I have not seen an example which did not carry the peacock's head. The various Queen's Ware examples (Plate 23) were displayed in Catalogue IX of 1882. By 1886, however, it was not selling well because of the high price and although the price had to be reduced the ware was a product of which the firm was proud. It is fairly dense, not easily chipped and some very good and unusual examples are still available. They all have a distinct charm but the two-handled dishes (Plate 24) require special mention because

of the delicate and complicated pattern and the excellent workmanship. Plate 25 shows a circular two-handled dish in Queen's ware which necessitated an extremely intricate and efficient mould pattern; the pattern being even more elaborate than shown in Plate 24.

The small vase (Plate 26) is also interesting. Portraying different Japanese figures on each of the four sides it was made to celebrate topically the popular Gilbert and Sullivan opera 'The Mikado', which was first produced in 1885. Queen's Ware is not always recognised by dealers in spite of its trade mark and characteristics. The tiny jug in Plate 23 was labelled 'Rockingham' when I bought it, presumably confusing the griffin mark with the Sowerby peacock head, and the Queen's Ware vase with the full decorative peacock pattern in Plate 14 was labelled 'Stourbridge' in an Antique Fair held in a five-star hotel with

very reputable dealers - where other items would not be questioned. This article carried a clear Sowerby trademark.

Some of the best moulds were kept for Queen's Ware articles and not used for other colours. Most Queen's Ware is a creamy colour, but I was interested to find two small articles in Queen's Ware which I thought had a distinctly greenish-yellow tinge such as uranium gives [30,31,32]. About a year later I had my opinion about this confirmed because I found a recipe for Queen's Ware, used after the original one, and the later one did indeed contain uranium. Queen's Ware was still being made in 1896, i.e. it was popular over at least 15 years.

An excellent appreciation of Queen's ware can be found [33]. This well-researched, comprehensive book covers the spectrum of Victorian glass throughout England, including the North-East. It gives sensitive assessments of these lovely wares.

TURQUOISE VITRO-PORCELAIN

The pale blue vitro-porcelain or slag ware (Plate 27 and see also Plate 19) has on occasion been called mistakenly 'King's Ware'. For example an editor of an American Antiques Journal in Massachusetts wrote to the Sowerby firm in 1928 asking if there was available any Vitro-porcelain glassware of Sowerbys, Queen's Ware, Malachite Ware and King's Ware'. There is however no evidence in the contemporary records about any King's Ware and it is of course highly unlikely that Sowerbys would have prejudiced their sales by giving any colour such a designation during Queen Victoria's reign. It would almost have been lese-majesty. Furthermore, the turquoise blue vitro-porcelain was produced in the late 1870's and was advertised as Turquoise in the Sowerby catalogue No. VIII i.e. before Queen's Ware which was advertised first in 1882 catalogue IX.

There is little doubt that the attractive hard-wearing pale blue ware was the Turquoise Vitro-porcelain alluded to in the early catalogues. The Oxford English Dictionary of 1961 tells us that turquoise is a precious stone of a 'sky blue to apple green colour, almost opaque'. Also that in 1753 Chambers Encyclopaedia described 'the pale blue of the natural turcois gem'; that in 1765 it was known that 'copper ... gives the turquoise colour to white glass'; that in 1882 the Ligurian Sea was described 'as blue as turquoise'; that in 1877 'beds of turquoise blue forget-me-nots' were noted and that the Daily News of the 15th July 1895 described how 'one of the ladies wore the beautiful turquoise blue of the season'. Additional evidence is to be found in a loose sheet discovered among the Sowerby records where the opal formula was given, and the same formula was used as a basis for both Queen's Ware and Turquoise (Fig. 4); the turquoise having copper scales added. Turquoise articles usually carry a peacock mark and were of top quality and imaginative design. There was a King's Ware much later after Queen Victoria's death but it was certainly not this Turquoise vitroporcelain which predated Queen's Ware.

BLANC DE LAIT GLASS (Plate 28. Two white slag parrot vases) ·

This glass is accurately described in its title being a dense pure white glass (see Plates 16 and 20). Opal glass which has a translucent watery-milk appearance and which has already been described (p.18) is sometimes confused with blanc de lait glass [34].

SHOE DESIGNS and OTHER ORNAMENTS

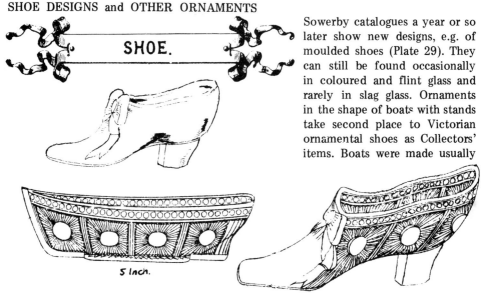

SHOE.

Sowerby catalogues a year or so later show new designs, e.g. of moulded shoes (Plate 29). They can still be found occasionally in coloured and flint glass and rarely in slag glass. Ornaments in the shape of boats with stands take second place to Victorian ornamental shoes as Collectors' items. Boats were made usually

5 Inch.

in two or three sizes and one stand would accommodate any size. Rather unattractive obelisk ornaments were also made.

RECEIPT FOR OPAL, QUEEN'S WARE AND TURQUOISE

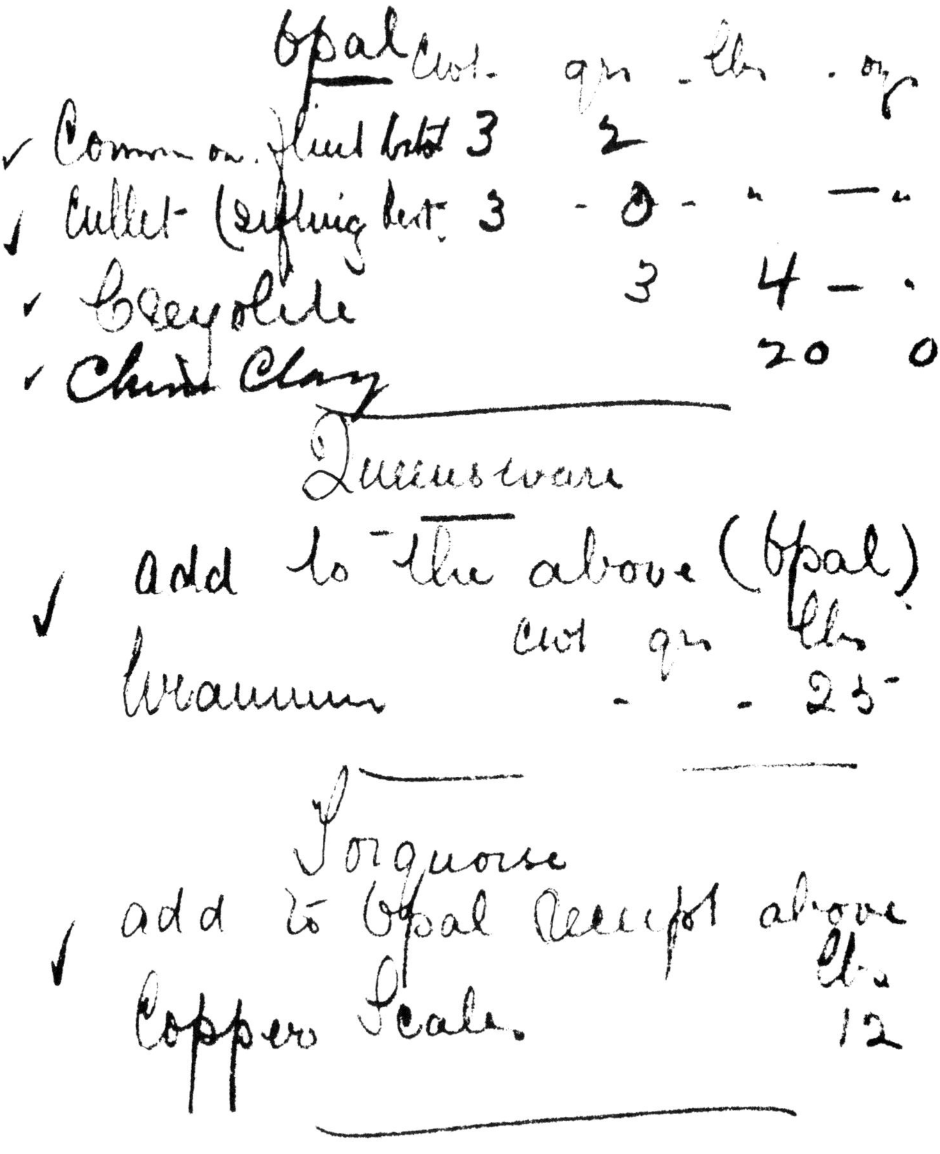

Opal cut. qrs. lbs. ozs.

✓ Common flint lots 3 2

✓ Cullet (sifting lot) 3 - 0 - " --"

✓ Cryolite 3 4 - .

✓ China Clay 20 0

Queensware

✓ add to the above (Opal)
 cwt qrs lbs
 Uranium - " - 25

Torquoise

✓ add to Opal Receipt above
 lbs
 Copper Scale. 12

Fig. 4

SWAN ORNAMENTS

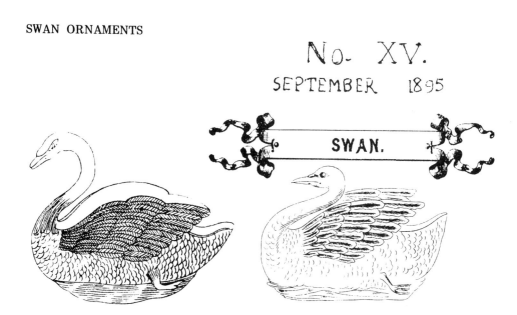

No. XV.
SEPTEMBER 1895

SWAN.

Handsome swan ornaments or sweetmeat dishes were popular. The neck, especially of the pattern shown on the left, is obviously fragile and not many have remained intact until the present time. An example in pale blue slag glass is shown in Plate 30.

THE DOLPHIN BOWL

An unusual pressed bowl called the dolphin bowl is shown in Plate 31. It is patterned round the sides, and stands on three feet which are three fishes heads whose bodies trail up the sides of the bowl. It is an amber colour at the base shading to such a deep intense red at the top of the bowl that a special place must be found for it in any collection because the colour overshadows other reds. It dates from about 1882, bears the Sowerby peacock and is unusual in showing the colour change from amber to red. This would have necessitated reheating the article to strike the colour, after pressing. It was also made in black, canary yellow, olive green and malachite colours and sometimes the bowl has been worked while hot into different shapes, e.g. square or indented. An experimental Dolphin bowl with crenated edge and different body patterns, and with a gold lustre surface treatment is shown in Plate 32 (see p.37 Iridiscent glass). Small candlesticks matching the amber/red bowl are also shown in Plate 31. The fitments for the candlesticks are recessed and not visible in the plate.

19th CENTURY RECIPES

In the Sowerby records of the 1880's a brief note described a coating on a gather of glass of black oxide of copper and black oxide of cobalt as being used for Antique glass for windows.

The records about ingredients of various batches were written in the same 19th Century style of handwriting as the Minutes but were 'peppered' with capital letters. which are reproduced here to preserve the effect.

Also in the 1880's there were five different blue colours used, which were Common Blue containing Zaffer i.e. an impure Oxide of Cobalt giving the blue pigment, Light Blue for fairy lamps, Blue for Casing with more cobalt, Celestial Blue containing Arsenic and Brass filings as well as Zaffer, and Germain Blue containing copper Vitrol.

Most of the good colours used were basically the Common Flint Batch with extra ingredients, e.g. Turquoise contained in addition to the Flint ingredients Cryolite, a Sodium aluminium fluoride, and oxide of Iron and Copper. A remark at the end of this recipe states, 'This is a good Turquoise and works well'.

Blue Malachite had Manganese added; Gold contained Oxide of Burnt Oats and Green had Oxide of Iron and Copper and Copper Scales added. Canary Colour was the Common Flint Batch, 4 cwts. 1qtr. in quantity with oxide Uranium 12 ozs. This produced 'a light colouration but a very good one'. Pomona Green (see p.16) was the same formula in different proportions, with oxide of copper added. In those days the cost of Canary colour for a batch was £3.14.0d, and from a batch the value of goods made and cullet left over was £7.8.7d. i.e. nearly 100% profit was made on each Canary colour batch.

A Black colour with Ground Coke but also with Dust coal added was recorded as known only to a few and that it was the dust coal 'that gives Brilliancy'. Plate 6 shows a brilliant Jet article.

For the Opal colour in 1888, 'Salt Peter, Fluor Spar, Fellspar and Arsenic' were added to the basic ingredients, but at a later date, probably about 1911, the opal was made by using 'Creyolite and China Clay' with the Common flint batch and sifted cullet. It was at this later time also that a new Queen's Ware was tried using this opal formula and to it adding 25 lbs. uranium (see p.29) but this gave in my opinion a rather inferior colour. Instructions for making the good early Queen's Ware were recorded on April 9th 1888 and advised as follows:- 'Melting cullets and watching it very closely, catching it before it burns itself out, and you get a very fair colour, or using a little batch made up with Opal Batch, and using with it 2 lbs. of yellow arsenic and you will have a good Queen's Ware'.

A colour called Opake also made in 1888 contained 2 lbs. clean siftings, 3 lbs. phosphate lime and 1 lb. arsenic. A footnote advised, 'If too opal, use less phosphate and 1 lb. more clean siftings'.

Puce, rated as a Common colour and sold at the same price as Flint and Common Green, was made merely by adding 1 lb. manganese to every Cwt. of Common Flint batch, but more care and trouble was taken with the Puce for Fairy Lamps, which had Arsenic also added. Puce colour was used as a basis for one of the first types of Iridescent glass produced by Sowerby's (see p. 40) which resulted in a bronze sheen. Flint batches were of course used for different purposes, for example one was especially made for 'Blowing Goods for Cutting', which contained a much smaller proportion of Lead than that used as the Flint Crystal Batch. Another formula between these two was stated to work well and cleanly and it was probably used as the basis for the coloured pressed articles as well as for the profusion of flint articles being produced over the same period (Plate 33).

The pioneer work on colours by J.G. Sowerby and the variety of adventurous patterns kept the Sowerby firm in the forefront until the end of the 19th Century.

FROM BOOK XI CRYSTAL TABLE GLASSWARE

(May 1st, 1885)

FROM BOOK XI May 1st 1885 continued

PLUG FOR JAR

35

FROM BOOK XI May 1st 1885 continued

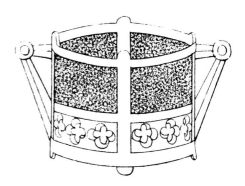

VENETIAN SERIES

All the articles described above are pressed goods but around the 1880's the Sowerby firm continued with some blown goods and produced their Venetian Series. This is a very desirable good quality blown glass either in flint colour or more attractively in a transparent but rather smoky green glass and both have pale blue opaque glass applied as edging or as thick threads around the rims and necks of jugs. They are artistically satisfying and a 'Venetian' green jug as catalogued in Book VIII of Sowerby & Co., is shown in Plate 34. The rare Venetian bowl of the same colour and with the same edging and with pale blue opaque prunts is not advertised in the same catalogue but clearly is of the same series. These wares are a lovely colour and good quality but they are rare and can be classed as museum pieces. Although examples in the Flint glass are rather heavy, the colour, styling, texture and 'delicacy' of the green Venetian wares explain the choice of this name for the series. They were made also in a transparent smoky brown glass, but I have seen only three such articles, a beaker and two small vases, none of which had the opaque blue 'threaded' decoration.

IRIDESCENT and CARNIVAL GLASS

A.C. Revi has done extensive research into the first commercial production of iridescent glass in the 19th Century, and he has carefully recorded the various early patents for such glass which were usually under the name of Iris or Rainbow glass. [26] Although the patent of Thomas Webb of Stourbridge in August 1877 for Iris Glass, to produce rainbow or prismatic tints, was not the first it followed closely on that of Ludwig Lobmeyer of Vienna and they both exhibited such glass in Paris in 1878. Plate 35 shows a blown Webb vase which bears the words 'Webb's Iris Glass' on the base and the iridescence is processed on to flint glass. This patent was quickly followed by that for Webb's Bronze Glass which also earned fulsome praise in 1878 from Queen Victoria who admired its bluish purple sheen which she likened to tempered steel or molten lead. Plate 36 shows two blown vases of Webb's Bronze glass with typical shapes. The main secret of this darker

VENETIAN. *Book VIII patterns*

VENETIAN.

Book VIII patterns

sheen was the use of a darker glass, a bluish-green, for the body of the article. Different chemical agents and innumerable changes in the detail of techniques produced the variations of iridescent glass from the many competing firms.

In the last two decades of the 19th Century the Sowerby firm produced some interesting pressed ware of good quality with the same surface treament. Plate 37 shows for example a sugar and cream set and a small bowl in a pattern from the 1885 catalogue, which has a gold lustre spread evenly over the article. Plate 38 shows a stemmed basin where the foot and stem of the article is in flint glass and the inside of the bowl has been treated and has resulted in Rainbow colours. Plate 39 shows a sugar and cream set, made from a sharply cut mould, which has an attractive bronze type lustre, where the body glass used was Puce colour. This carries the peacock trademark and is probably from the 1880's or earlier. These articles are interesting historically showing the production techniques used in attempting to compete at the time with the handmade articles of other firms. In the 20th Century techniques for iridescence became more stereotyped and a profusion of Carnival glass was produced (see p.54 et seq).

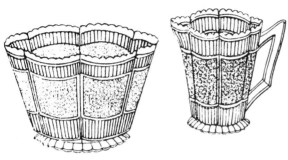

May 1st 1885

In the late 19th Century the covered area of the Sowerby firm in East Street excluding the vast warehouses occupied three acres of space at Gateshead; the staff employed numbered nearly three hundred; all of the iron work for making the moulds and presses was done on the premises, and there were nine furnaces. In spite of claims to the contrary not all Sowerby articles of the 1880's bear the trademark and registration number. Many do not. It is, however, true that their most expensive wares, e.g. Queen's Ware, usually did carry the trademark. The building in East Street is still in the hands of the present owners, the Suntex Group of Companies, but coloured art glass is no longer produced there.

In 1888 the firm had world wide renown, and their catalogue of the time proclaimed new offices in Amsterdam and Brussels in addition to those previously mentioned. It continued to produce glass of immense variety and popular patterns.

When I first became acquainted with the firm in 1969, coloured pressed glass was still being manufactured, and I was privileged to see an old-fashioned pot setting which was done at working temperatures, for the pot had been worked that morning. My notes written shortly after the event record that the pot weighed one ton and was set by a team of nine men. It was an unforgettable occasion because of the air of drama and danger in the operation. The fierce heat and the sweaty excitement of the men, who covered their arms with shields to protect their faces, set the scene. The hats, goggles, wet gloves and implements, along with the showmanship of pulling away the bricks and spearing the pot free continued the act, and then the old pot looking like a red hot elephant was finally removed from the furnace, placed on its 'iron carriage' and wheeled triumphantly away through the glassworks, to accompanying screams and shouts of the volunteer team. A second wave of excitement occurred when the new pot pre-heated to white-heat, was wheeled in and manoeuvred expertly into place by the team. This would be allowed to settle in, be worked up to critical temperature and tried two or three days later. The leader of the team was well satisfied with their performance and said to me, "Every pot is different and each one is a new challenge." They were allowed a drink and a rest and two hours were put on to their week's pay.

I was struck by the great similarity of the event to the description of a pot setting written in 1849 more than 100 years earlier by Apsley Pellatt [35] in his book of 1849 'Curiosities of Glass Making' which described graphically what I saw. 'The old pot, being no longer useful, by age or accident, is then exposed, by pulling down the temporary brickwork, a large iron bar, steeled and sharpened at the point, is placed across another bar, to operate under the pot as a fulcrum; several men rest their entire weight upon the end of this long lever, and after one or many efforts and perhaps many more simultaneous blows of the bar, used as a sort of battering ram - the old pot either wholly or in pieces, is detached from the siege of the furnace.'

'About six or eight men take afterwards each a bar about five feet long, like a javelin steeled and sharpened at one end; they rush forward in face of the fiery furnace, guarding their faces with their protected arms, and aim a blow at such of the irregular rocky incrustations of clay as adhere to the siege. This operation is repeated until the pieces of partially vitrified clay are wholly removed from the position on which the old pot stood, which should be repaired with clay and sand. The new pot, at a white heat, is then removed from the annealing pot-arch, and carried upon the end of a two-wheeled iron carriage with a long handle by four or more workmen, who carefully set it or tilt it backwards into its proper position in the furnace .... The fatigue and exhaustion of the men, who are often detained four hours in this operation, is also very great, and is attended occasionally by severe falls, burns, or bruises, by liability to catch cold, great excitement, energetic exertion, and exposure to the flame of the open furnace.'

Looking back, I think it was the last rites of the Industrial Revolution which we attended. How lucky we were to see it.

The last pot has been set and the last furnace has gone out at the Sowerby firm after a very long history, for glass production has ceased at the works which undertakes, at present, only the cutting and fabrication of car windscreens in that particular building. Some of the intervening period for which there are records, from the late 19th Century up to the present are covered in the following account.

Selections from 1885 Price List and Catalogue XI
and a Continuation Book XI

11 INCH BOWL ON CELERY
OBSCURED AND PLAIN

CANDLE ORNAMENTS

in Bright and Colored Glass

42

*Selections from 1885 Price List and Catalogue XI
and a Continuation of Book XI*

QUART AND PINT

Selections from

Pattern Book.

No. XV. SEPTEMBER, 1895.
No. XVI. JANUARY, 1898.

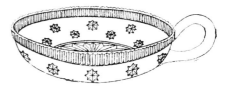

*Selections from Pattern Book No. XV September, 1895
and No. XVI January, 1898 continued and Book XIX*

12 INCH

BIRD FURNITURE.

All articles were drawn one-third the actual size.

THE DAWN OF THE 20th CENTURY

By late 1891 the firm was in financial difficulties, serious losses were occurring in the bottle department, the bank overdraft was at the allowed limit of £5,000 and the manager was wondering how to provide the wages due. A decision was taken to close the bottle department, to put all workmen on to half time and not to make any goods except for orders. Three months later a miners' strike worsened the position, notice was given that all engagements would terminate in two weeks and re-engagement would be only from day to day and the bank kept a tight hold threatening a 10% interest charge in the event of 'unpunctuality of payment'. In spite of these difficulties, business was still brisk during 1892 and 241 moulds with new designs were made while 97 were made to replace old designs.

Mr. Henry Harley Pitt, the foreman in the Sowerby mould room in 1892, patented a new steam press machine. He was given permission to try it, it was successful and he was offered a hire of his machine at £10 per month and a royalty of 5% on the sale of goods made by the machine. It was agreed that machines would also be offered to Messrs. G. Davidson & Co., E. Moore & Co., Greener & Co., M. Turnbull & Co., Sowerby & Co., Lemington and Allen & Co., i.e. all the local glassworks, but Sowerby's Ellison Glassworks Ltd., were to have first offer of patent rights if Mr. Pitt wanted to dispose of these.

In 1896 a patent was taken out for a new Glory Hole in the joint names of Mr. H.H. Pitt and the Company, and an agreement was later signed and sealed to transfer to the Company all of Mr. Pitt's patents for his press and Glory Hole and any improvements connected therewith. These details are recorded because subsequently the machine and patents became the subject of a lengthy legal case between the Company and H.H. Pitt. A year later, Mr. J.G. Sowerby had to resign because of ill-health and he was replaced by Mr. H.H. Pitt as Manager.

Meanwhile many alterations had been made in the Ellison Factory - new mixing machines were bought, the cut warehouse was done away with, cutting being done only to order, a storage tank for liquid fuel was installed and power was suggested instead of hand labour to bring coal from the railway sidings into the depot.

At this time the Sowerby firm was known throughout the world; it had representatives in many countries and was aware of its competitors, for example the Company decided not to exhibit at the Brussels Exhibition in 1897 because there was too short a time to prepare samples to do the company credit 'especially alongside the exhibit of Val St. Lambert'.

Early in 1896 Sowerby's purchased land near Antwerp and erected a new factory at Hoboken, Belgium, but in February 1897 news was received by wire that the new factory had been blown down by a hurricane of unusual violence. Hoboken was never a project that really flourished; rebuilding took place but other difficulties arose and although the books of the Societé Anonyme des Cristalleries de Hoboken were in good order, the Hoboken factory struggled on, but closed eventually in 1907.

In the Sowerby Pattern Book No. XVI dated January 1898 there were patterns very much as before and nothing new which was very noteworthy.

Selections from a Continuation of Book XI

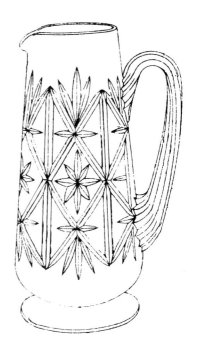

Selections from a Continuation of Book XI

AMERICAN SETS.

Butter, Round.

Sugar & Cover.

Spoon Holder.

Milk.

BOOK XIX   JUNE 1907

SOWERBY (iii)

20th CENTURY ELLISON WORKS

In February 1900 through the Town Clerk of Newcastle, His Excellency the Minister Plenipotentiary of China proposed a visit to Newcastle and wished to visit the Ellison Works. Permission was granted, but unfortunately no colourful details were given on this visit, although it does emphasise the firm's wide renown.

Late in 1900 the first inkling of trouble with Mr. H.H. Pitt arose. A deputation of the glassworkers complained of slackness of work compared to other works in the neighbourhood, and they stated that too much attention was being given to Pitt's Patent Glory Hole. One of the Directors suspected Mr. Pitt's management of the works and requested that another Director superintend the mixing of the metal, suggest new colours and patterns and report on the management of the glasshouse monthly. There is the first inkling also that the ascendancy of the Sowerby firm is about to wane somewhat for Mr. T. Davidson of the rival firm is the Chairman of the Northern Association of Pressed Glass Manufacturers.

Complaints rather than praise became usual, for example a complaint was received from Meredith and Drew, a valued customer in London, about faulty Sowerby goods received, and 'Mr. Pitt had to admit that they were very bad indeed'. Orders on hand were cancelled and the account closed. Also in 1901, the Sunbeam Lamp Co., complained about the quality of electric bulbs which the Sowerby Company was supplying and the standard of the work generally seems to have fallen. Messrs. Hoffning & Co., of Australia, the largest shippers and dealers of glass in the colonies, considered American glass to be cheaper and infinitely better in quality than Greener's glass or Sowerby's, and that second in quality was Davidson's glass although prices were too high. Difficulties were arising both with Mr. Pitt, who prolonged a visit to the Hoboken works unduly, and with the latter works because an official intimation of failure had been received and the Societé became bankrupt.

In August 1902 there was a great scarcity of orders but the Directors' minutes optimistically read that 'now the coronation holidays are over' perhaps things will improve. The Victorian era had ended; Edward VII was King.

EDWARDIAN ERA

Early in 1905 Mr. Percival Marson from Stourbridge offered the Sowerby company a recipe for 'Straw Ruby' glass gathered from the pot. He declared that it had not been sold to any other person and he wanted £5 if a trial was successful, £10 on goods being made out of metal and 1% up to £1,000 thereafter. He enclosed 'a sample of green striking yellow and ruby' without charge, promised the recipe in a day or so and offered to submit all further colours likely to be of use and generally to advise them in this sphere. He asked to know their terms and stated that 'of course it is essential that I should know your standard receipts to put me on a proper foundation to adapt further colours'. The firm accepted the terms re the Straw Ruby colour but did not commit themselves further at this stage. More than six months later Mr. Pitt had not succeeded with the recipe and

Mr. Marson was asked to attend the works to assist in making the colours wanted. After further delay Mr. Pitt stated he had been unable to progress due to illness but in late October he submitted samples of Straw Ruby for inspection, but even then he 'hoped to make the colour saleable with slight alterations in the metal and new methods of fire polishing'. In November the colour was at last a success and new moulds for 1906 were pushed forward, but the selected name 'Sunglow' for this colour proved not to be possible. This long development of a proven recipe gives some justification for the present high prices of this type of glass shading to Ruby and also of the so called 'Cranberry Glass'. (See Plate 40).

Consternation occurred in January 1906 when the Sowerby foreman allowed two strangers into the glasshouse, one of whom was discovered the following day to be the mould room foreman of Messrs. Greener & Co., a rival firm at Sunderland. The Sowerby foreman was immediately suspended but, after an apologetic letter regretting his mistake, was reinstated.

Unfortunate news came in a letter from the South American agent of a serious earthquake in 'Valpaaiso' resulting for him in two months work wasted, for trial orders were of no use 'as many of the clients were dead and any living were absolutely ruined by the fire and earthquake.'

It was apparent from the records that Mr. Pitt was repeatedly making excuses for poor trade and poor management and always promising that manufacturing profits would be increased, often regretting bad balances, low selling prices, glassmakers limiting output due to Whit holidays, Race holidays and new systems of working, etc. In September 1906 'owing to the intense heat he had not been able to drive the furnaces as he would have liked. Several stoppages arose owing to boys fainting, etc., and they were obliged to go home'.

A month later Mr. Pitt was explaining an unfortunate accident when two of the screwbolts in the middle tie-band of a furnace stripped and, in flying off, struck the top band which also flew off. The top part of the furnace expanded to such an extent that both the crown and chimney fell through the furnace. The cost of rebuilding was £20 and there was a great delay in executing orders. This distressing news was followed by the absence of Mr. Pitt through illness and his medical adviser, who thought overwork to be the main cause of the illness, recommended a complete change.

Mr. Pitt therefore sailed for America and two weeks later cabled laconically 'Well'. He had asked if he might try to sell the recipe for 'Sunglow' glass in America, goods of this colour made at the 'Ellison' were not selling well because of price, but permission had not been granted. On returning three weeks later Adam Dodds, the Secretary, agreed to work jointly with Mr. Pitt so that the latter's anxieties would be lessened. The Directors had been well pleased with the recent management of the works by the Secretary during Mr. Pitt's absence.

With Mr. Pitt, acting jointly as Manager in 1907 but still causing concern and unease to, and provoking criticism from, the Board about his performance there is a gap in the Directors' records, but H.H. Pitt left the Company during 1907 and in 1912 Sowerby's obtained the verdict with costs against him in the Chancery Court. Sowerby's the Plaintiffs, claimed the return of a model and drawings relating to a blast furnace for the manufacture of glass. Mr. Justice Neville's opinion was that the defendant had acquired his knowledge of the furnace whilst in Belgium for the benefit of the plaintiffs and was not entitled to exploit it in this country among other glass manufacturers. The judge ordered delivery up of the drawings to the plaintiffs and granted an injunction restraining the defendant from making use of any model or drawings of the plaintiff's furnace. Mr. Pitt had meanwhile gone to the nearby Davidson firm on a five-year contract. His tenure as Manager at Sowerby's had been disastrous. He was a tall, fresh-coloured man, and unpopular with the mould makers, being considered bombastic, he did not serve the full time with the Davidson firm.

From 1907 after the departure of Harold H. Pitt, Adam Dodds provided successful management at Sowerby's. He had been connected with many sports and in 1911 a solid silver loving bowl was subscribed for by over 150 well-known sportsmen and commercial representatives. His first athletic success was in a sprint race at the age of 17 years. He was connected with Rugby football, became a member of North Durham Cricket Club, for 12 years acting as Chairman, won a Worsdale cup for bowls, was an adept hand at quoits, indulged in tennis, played billiards well and finally fell for golf. He was an excellent raconteur and a true and trusty friend. So stated Mr. Tom Davidson making the presentation, continuing that it was no secret that the resurrection of the Sowerby Ellison Glassworks from 'an apparently decaying concern into an active one was largely due to Adam Dodds'. The severe reverses of the Sowerby firm had been of comparatively short duration but for many further years the Davidson firm was in the ascendancy and Tom Davidson was the outstanding personality. He and Adam Dodds were great friends, with horse racing as a shared enthusiasm.

The Sowerby Pattern book of June 1907 No. XIX has a different look to previous catalogues. There are less fussy designs and in particular the Ruby sugar and cream (No. 2230) set is plain and unadorned. There is no ribbing or applied flint decoration.

Sugar, Ruby.

Sugar, Ruby.

Cream, Ruby

In January 1912 a play entitled RUTHERFORD AND SON written by K.G. Sowerby was produced at the Royal Court Theatre, London.* It was hailed as the most powerful play produced in England in a decade and the Daily Chronicle reported that the audience were thundering in vain for the author's appearance. It was not immediately known that K.G. Sowerby was a woman and this seemed to add to the interest when it was discovered. She was the grand-daughter of John Sowerby who owned the glassworks in East Street and the daughter of John G. Sowerby, the artist.

The play's story is one of the tyranny of the head of a glassworks who crushes his men and has little humanity. His daughter meets the foreman of the works, a worshipper of the master's power and the play is drawn around these three characters. It serves to emphasise the historical status and importance of glass owners at the turn of the century when they were men of stature and substance.

RUTHERFORD AND SON, Act I, is introduced as follows :-

'John Rutherford's house stands on the edge of the moor, far enough from the village to serve its dignity and near enough to admit of the master going to and from the works in a few minutes - a process known to the household as 'going across'. The living room is furnished in solid mahogany and papered in red, as if to mitigate the bleakness of a climate that includes five months of winter in every year ....'

At the end of March 1912 the play was still running and was described by London Opinion as 'a useful money spinner' and 'A remarkable play, grey even to gloominess but strong as steel'. The American rights were sold and the play was translated into German and French. Miss Githa Kate Sowerby lived with her sister Millicent and for years she had been writing children's stories, reputed to be exquisite tales, which her sister illustrated. The photographs of Kate Sowerby showed her as a goodlooking, fashionably dressed personable young lady, and the Daily Mail 5th February 1912 described her as, 'tall, fair, with a pretty face and a very pleasant voice'. Sometimes at rehearsal the producer would ask her what some line or phrase meant. She would reply, "Why should I know any more about them than anybody else? There they are, walking about and saying all these things. That's really all I know about them".

A second play, 'Before Breakfast', had a successful premiere two or three months later, by when she had become engaged to a colleague, Captain John Kendall, author of the comedy 'Mrs. Bill' and of a one act play produced at Drury Lane in 1910 called 'Laughter in Court'. Kate Sowerby's third play 'A Man and Some Women' was somewhat disappointing but in 1916 another was more successful - a comedy called 'Sheila' in which Fay Compton appeared.

Also in 1912 Alderman Weidner, who was one of the Sowerby Directors, bought Coupland Castle, a fine old historic mansion near Wooler from the turrets of which there was a magnificent view of Flodden Field. Alderman Weidner was appointed Lord Mayor for the City of Newcastle for the year 1914.

In 1912 to 1914 high Sowerby sales were recorded and a monthly sales record of £4,471 was reached in June 1914 which was the highest since mid-1883 when under J.G. Sowerby the amount was £4,815. This rosy picture was soon darkened by the outbreak of the first World War.

* This play was re-enacted at the Royal Court Theatre, London in April 1980

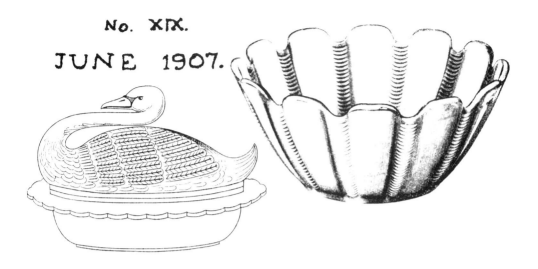

No. XIX.

JUNE 1907.

FIRST WORLD WAR

The first entry about the event reads, 'Intense excitement created by the War. Men enlisting and time lost owing to pals enrolling, managing the men is difficult. Without any further supplies, I think we can carry on for about three months longer'. Immediately the obtaining of sand became a major problem. While all the time hoping to obtain supplies as usual from Fontainbleu, samples from New York, Sweden, Belgium, Ireland, King's Lynn and locally were tried but none was found suitable, in fact they were considered to be 'very inferior indeed' to French sand and the Glass Technology Department of Sheffield University confirmed that 'Fontainbleu sand stands first, with Dutch if properly treated a good second'. Soon after, a small steamer left Rouen with 280 tons of sand, half of which was destined for the Sowerby firm. In 1915 in association with Sheffield University the glass manufacturers of the North and Midlands formed a Society of Glass Technology.

At M. Turnbull & Co., a local firm, and at Davidson's Works the men worked night and day, but at Sowerby's they refused to work at night time because 'lads' were not available although, during the war, boy labour was allowed from 13 years of age instead of 14 years of age. A sorry tale of trade difficulties at Sowerby's followed, travellers were taken off the road because the firm could not execute orders; there was a scarcity of straw for packing, and habitual drunkards in the works were a cause of trouble.

In mid-1916 apprentices made excellent goods of a certain class during a lengthy stoppage of work by glassmakers which was not settled until a whole year later in mid-1917. Although this was followed by an 'abundance of orders' and the glassmakers working extremely well, by the start of 1918 they were on strike yet again over wages and the Ministry of Munitions of War tried to arrange a settlement.

In June 1918 the Sowerby Manchester representative joined the colours, the office closed because the assistant Secretary and wages Clerk were called up and the showroom was kept open only with the charwomen and the sample cleaner.

In July 1918 the men insisted on increases in wages of 28% and 'other conditions favourable to themselves'. The general opinion was that some automatic pressing machinery from America was the only way to deal with the position. The whole of the six works in the Northern Association of Pressed Glass Manufacturers were affected and Adam Dodds with Mr. Tom Davidson visited the Minister of Munitions of War in Piccadilly, but there was to be no settlement of the strike until September 1918.

Two Decades Between the Wars

In January 1919 the glassmakers started to come back out of the Army one by one, and in March 1919 Adam Dodds wrote that the increased prices of Sowerby goods were known 'from the mixing room to the office boy (who, as you know, is a woman about 50 years old) and in consequence there are demands for larger increases in wages'. In the same year Adam Dodds visited America and found that in Pittsburg the tumblers were not good enough for Sowerby's, but that in Toledo the Libbey Glass Company and the Modern Glass Co., 'make beautiful goods, superior to ours and mostly for cutting. I did not see in the shops or in hotels anything to compete with the North of England but of course there were some articles seen which were very superior and expensive and made only for the few'. Exclusive engravings by Joseph Locke, wares by Louis Comfort Tiffany and by Frederick Carder were probably being referred to. Adam Dodds returned to Gateshead and to his glasswork worries and the details of glasshouse management. For example an anonymous letter in 1919 read, 'Dear Sir, I am sending you this letter to let you know about the women you have working for you. They are carrying loads of glass out every night at 5 o'clock so you can look out for them. They have buckets under their striks (sic). From a one who has bought some'. A fire due to a spark from a glory hole spread rapidly because of the antiquated roof of the works and an iron roof was eventually substituted. Adam Dodds arranged purchase of a horse at a cost of £115, choosing a horse for delivering goods from a firm already doing some work for Sowerby's because the horse was well known to Sowerby staff.

In the years after the First World War, competition from abroad was severe and 'there were original designs of beautiful quality and vivid colouring coming especially from France'. These must have been the Cameo vases of Gallé, Daum, Legras, Arsale, and other colleagues. The glass of René Lalique was also famed, and the Sowerby records concede less demand for the contemporary British semi-transparent alabaster glass in delicate colourings of pink, blue or green, and this was very inferior in style and texture.

CARNIVAL GLASS

In the twentieth Century techniques for producing a surface golden lustre on glass became standardised and the particular advantages and cheapness of pressing were exploited. By the nineteen twenties and thirties large amounts of this cheap lustred ware were produced. This is Carnival Glass - so called because it was frequently used as give-away prizes at Carnivals and fairs. Most Carnival glass has a light golden and often a very thin lustre on the surface but other sheens and colour effects were produced and are rated differently by Collectors, Green and Blue Carnival ware being the most rare. Some of the gold lustre articles are of very poor quality but others are good. Different patterns were moulded, e.g. the thistle pattern, the rose pattern, etc., and as other old glass becomes more scarce, this Carnival glass seems to be gaining in popularity. (In contrast, see earlier iridescent or lustre glass p 37).

SOWERBY TYNESYDE GLASSWARE

"TYNESYDE" GLASSWARE

LIST No. 36

In 1922, Sowerby's Tyne Glass was launched, the symbol of the Tyne Bridge was used in advertising and a round scallop-edged black paper label with gold lettering and gold edging bore the words 'Sowerby's Tynesyde Glassware'.

"TYNESYDE"   LIST No. 36

According to the records a new book of advanced patterns helped trade considerably so that cut work of pre-war days was re-introduced. The glass was a crystal which the firm boasted 'competes with all opposition at home or abroad', and it claimed, 'Every penny spent on Tyne Glass goes to pay Tyneside work-people wages'. (See Plates 41, 42, 43). About 400 people were now em-ployed in the firm. In 1923 and 1924, Percival Marson, whose first approach to the Company had been 15 years earlier, was now the Company's Chemist, and usually sporting leggings and a white coat, was busy with new colours which materially helped to sell the goods. Some Tynesyde Glass was produced in amber, blue and green, and in a much advertised 'Rosalin' shade. Two examples of special coloured Tynesyde ware were the 'Ladye' powder bowl in pastel shades, acid finished (see Fig. 5) and the 'Flora' series of a bowl and figure, and a vase and flower holder - both of these were advertised in separate leaflets with five-colour printing. But money became scarce and even the best customers took extended credit. The value of goods manufactured during 1925 was Flint £41,921, Sunglow and Rainbow £12,643 and Ruby £3,192. Certain work in colours in an experimental stage was payable at a special rate. A new furnace was purchased which could be worked at considerably

6 2593 SALAD BOWL, Hexagonal, 8½". Flint

increased heat but 'therein lay danger' according to the manager because four pots were broken at an early stage - 'Teasers will have to understand the difference more thoroughly before we are out of trouble', he wrote.

Some of the Tynesyde articles were of good quality and of typical Art Deco style.

In 1925 the local glass industry had the quietest time it had experienced for many years and the Glassmakers Association applied to the Board of Trade for 'protection'. In fact the general election of 1923 had been fought on the industrial question of 'Protection of British Industries'. Heavy dues were levied on British goods going abroad and the only export trade left was to the British Colonies, Australia, New Zealand and South Africa. 'Protection' amounted to goods coming into Britain having to pay the same duty as goods going abroad. This, however, did not apply to glassware which was pressed, and consequently the market was flooded with pressed glass made in America, Holland, Belgium, Czechoslovakia, Japan, and to a greater extent than ever before, Germany. All of these goods came into this country free of tax. In 1926 'Sunglow Lustre Glassware' was advertised as a specialty and also black, opal, ruby and other coloured goods, but during 1926 sales fell to no less than £12,222 nett below the previous year, these conditions being created by the miners' strike following a long period of depression. In mid-1927 the manager was at his wits' end to improve matters. Competition from the continent was fierce and dumping continued with frequent reports of blank days from the travellers. A large buyer of English glass told how a foreign firm's traveller called with stocks of a good line. The traveller had no fixed price but said, "If you buy the lot you can have them at your own price". The goods were bought and delivered immediately.

Encouragement was given to local trade as evidenced by a report in the Morning Post of 22nd February 1925. An entry read, "The Queen visited the British Industries Fair again yesterday accompanied by the Duke and Duchess of York and the Princess Royal. The Queen bought something at almost every stall she inspected and the number was considerable. It is estimated that Her Majesty now has walked over 80 miles at British Industries Fairs'.

Adam Dodds, during all these years, was a dedicated manager, very conscientious, worried by the poor health of his wife and somehow over-dedicated to the Company. He allowed his own car to be used to travel the Border towns with satisfactory results

3

MADE IN PASTEL SHADES OF AMBER, GREEN, BLUE and ROSALIN. ACID FINISH.

 SOWERBY'S ELLISON GLASSWORKS LTD.

Fig. 5

and the firm eventually decided to buy a small car. A Morris Oxford was tried out one Sunday, the trial consisting of Mr. Dodds' man driving 278 miles with five adults! The asking price was £175 for a late 1926 model, strongly leather-covered, which had belonged previously to a Solicitor who was getting a more powerful car.

1928 ended and 1929 began with Adam Dodds much troubled by the illness of his wife but predicting that 1929 would be an improvement because of new novel goods of advanced pattern. This is the last report written in the full, flowing, dated handwriting, carefully penned by Adam Dodds for in March 1929 his death at the age of 70 years was announced with the deepest regret.

In the beautifully written reports which must have taken many hours to write it is interesting to note that Adam Dodds talked of a furnace as female. Having decided that it was necessary to put one out he continued, "I fully expect to have her repaired to begin working again soon".

After reading his many reports, one could almost imagine his reflective pause after writing a short sad minute in 1905, 'On Saturday 28th October the horse died suddenly, age 20 years, 15 of which she worked for the Company'. Likewise, 'The London and South East Traveller was at last run to ground and his resignation readily accepted. Motoring with a lady supposed to be his wife and also reported to have carried China contrary to agreement'!

In July 1913 the output of one furnace was 55,678 lbs weight which certainly constituted a record in the Ellison Works, if not in the whole trade throughout England. Adam Dodds was something of a father figure - for example, one entry of his states, 'The glassmakers have not worked so well since Bank Holiday. The fact is they are making too much money and many of them have not the sense to take care of it. I am dealing with the question as well as I can'.

In October 1917 he had installed electric light into the offices, 'and made provision for extensions which owing to the bad quality of gas are sure to be needed shortly'. His bi-monthly reports made frequent allusions to the drinking habits of the glassmakers and displayed in the scrapbook as an 'Object Lesson' was a newspaper cutting about a workman who for 'illegally absenting himself from the City Glass Bottle Co. Ltd., at West Ham,' was ordered to forfeit £10 or serve 31 days imprisonment. 'The firm on Government work had been greatly inconvenienced through heavy drinking on the part of some workers'. Two Sowerby workers were fined rather more modestly 40/- and 9/6d. for absenting themselves, one pleaded that he was getting on in years and the other said his son had come from the front and he had had a drink or two.

An entry in the scrapbook is of topical interest. 'A letter from the Gateshead Works, Post Office stamped 9.0 p.m., 5th June 1923 was delivered at 19 Basinghall Street, London E.C. at 8.0 a.m. 6th June 1923. It was thought worthy of the Album to record that another letter had been sent at 5.30 p.m. on 5th June - comment in red ink stated, 'Both letters delivered at same time, 8.0 a.m.' Fifty years later I am wondering whether the remark was condemnatory about the second letter or praising the speedy delivery of the first. I can only marvel at the service then given, as I have done all through these reports about the world wide arrangements, communications and contacts of the Sowerby firm.

The large numbers of letters received on the death of Adam Dodds who was 50 years with the Company showed the respect in which he had been held throughout the trade. He was followed by J.R. Lauderdale as Works Manager.

At the British Industries Fair at Olympia in February 1932 Queen Mary and the Duke and Duchess of York, pleased with the beauty and finish of the Sowerby articles ordered a number of purchases, while in 1934 the comment in the Journal of the Newcastle and Gateshead Chamber of Commerce was 'that the Queen managed to walk seven miles in the hot atmosphere of Olympia was another example of Her Majesty's determination to further the interests of her subjects.'

In the 1935 Exhibition, Queen Mary's purchases of 30 pieces at the Sowerby's Ellison Glassworks stall included a 'Squirrel' fruit bowl, a sugar and cream set, and other pieces in various colours and a fruit bowl in white glass. One of the moulds in use had been made in the time of J.G. Sowerby. In her turn Queen Elizabeth the Queen Mother carried on the habit, and chose and purchased several Sowerby pieces of glass at various B.I.F. Exhibitions, which were held each February.

1939 and post Second World War

The Second World War in 1939 brought practical agreements with the workers as to how payments should be calculated when production was interrupted due to Air Raid Alerts.

Sowerby's produced the notable pink tinted glassware called 'Rosalin' before the 1939 War but because of difficulties with supplies it appeared again only in 1954 in the B.I.F. of that year.

In 1940 orders were exectued by Sowerby's for goods for the prestigious Queen Mary, then the largest liner afloat.

In 1948 the Revd. R.J. Green, a son-in-law of the late J.G. Sowerby became Chairman of the Sowerby Company and in 1949 J.R. Lauderdale retired as Managing Director after twenty years in this role. He was 6' 3" in height, a bachelor who lived with his married sister, and he had proved to be a hard but just employer. A presentation Dinner at the Royal Station Hotel was arranged and the menu was appropriately :-

> Hors d'oeuvres Sowerby Ellison
> Poulet a la Jobling
> Pommes Teams.   Harricot Verts Purser
> Canape Knottingley
> Cafe Davidson

The local glass manufacturers had rallied and the various courses related to one or other of the local glassworks:- Sowerby's Ellison Glassworks, James A Jobling Ltd., the Teams Glassworks of G. Davidson & Co., and Messrs. Hagley Glassworks of Knottingley, Yorkshire.

In March 1956, Debenture holders of the Sowerby firm appointed a Receiver for the Company who decided that the business should carry on trading while efforts were made to sell it as a going concern or to make new arrangements. In January 1957, the workers expected dismissal but a last minute reprieve was granted when a well known firm of glass manufacturers expressed interest, and in March 1957 Sowerby's was taken over on an individual basis by Mr. Jack Davis, Managing Director of Suntex Safety Glass Ind. Ltd. and Associated Companies of the Suntex Estate of Iver, Bucks. The intention was that production on the same lines would continue, for he wanted to retain the famous name in the glass industry and to carry on the traditional trade of Sowerby's Ellison Glassworks. But the last production of coloured fancy glass was in March 1972, when the valves of the furnace in East Street at the Ellison Works were turned off for the last time, and the coloured glass interests passed to the Nazing Glassworks near London. I hold one of the last articles to have come out of the Sowerby pots.

Thus, with an illustrious history reaching back at least to the early 19th Century, the Sowerby firm reached its zenith in the years 1876 to 1900 mainly because of the enthusiasm, artistry and flair of J.G. Sowerby and his experimental work with colours for glass. After his departure, under the management of H.H. Pitt, the firm lost its renown and although the efforts of Adam Dodds and others restored commercial success it never again achieved its former fame when the peacock was the proud trademark of the Sowerby firm in the 1870's and 1880's. The surviving examples of the interesting Sowerby glass of that time are now greatly sought after by collectors and are something to be proud of and treasured.

It is not yet too late for Museums to rectify the situation and acquire really good examples of the early pressed work of J.G. Sowerby, for some are still available and in perfect condition even though 100 years old or more.

J. G. SOWERBY, THE ARTIST

Plates 44 and 45 show two watercolours by J.G. Sowerby, both in the Author's Collection.

The style of the figures in 'The Summons' is very similar to some of the book illustrations done by J.G. Sowerby e.g. in 'At Home' (Marcus Ward & Co. London 1881) and 'Afternoon Tea' (1880). A recent sale at Sotheby's has contained a delicate watercolour by J.G. Sowerby, entitled The Milkmaid.

Plate 1   Sowerby Purple Malachite Ware from 1872 to 1882. Largest article c. 1872
11.5 cm across top, 8 cm high. All with Peacock trademark.

Plate 2   Sowerby Purple Malachite candlesticks. Pattern 1311 c. 1885. Peacock
trademark 23.5 cm high.

Plate 3   Crinolined·lady in Marble slag glass,
probably American. 9.5 cm high.

Plate 4   Sowerby Malachite stemmed
            basin, 14 cm top diam., 14 cm high

Plate 8   Early Sowerby Opal Vase, April
            1879. 9 cm high, 5 cm square
            Peacock trademark.

Plate 5   Sowerby Green Malachite ornament c. 1877. 3 cm. high.

Plate 9   Sowerby Opal double salt c. 1880, 10 cm length, Peacock mark.

Plate 10   Sowerby Opal Swan Vase
c. 1879. 9.5 cm high.

Plate 11   'Siren's' Plate marked R. LALIQUE
FRANCE No. 3003. 17.5 cm diam.

Plate 12   Sowerby green vase decorated with white filaments c. 1880. Pattern no. 1244, 7 cm high.

Plate 14   Queen's Ware Peacock vase c. 1882. 5.5 cm high and Turquoise Font Vase c. 1877, 10 cm high.

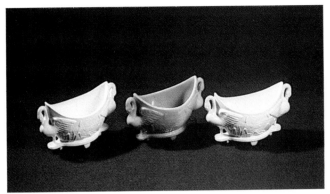

Plate 15   Three Swan vases with Peacock head trademark. Each is 13 cm long axis,
8 cm high.

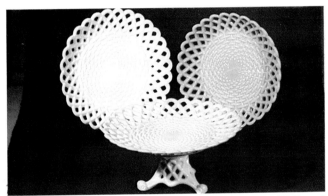

Plate 17   Turquoise blue basket weave plate on stand, 21.5 cm. White and green
basket weave plates.

Plate 19   Jack & Jill vases, 9 cm high and Vase No. 1269   8.5 cm high. All with
Peacock trademark.

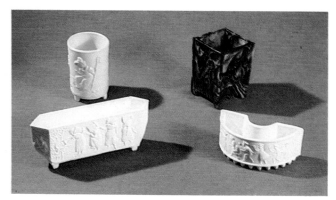

Plate 20   Examples of Rhyme or Nursery Themes in Queen's Ware, Turquoise, Blanc de Lait & Purple Malachite, 11 cm long axis posy vase.

Plate 21   2 hand-painted Blanc de Lait bowls, one on four feet c. 1879, 8 cm high; other c. 1880, 6 cm high and small hand-gilded vase c. 1877, 8 cm high. All with Peacock trademark.

Plate 22   Early Opal bowl hand-painted in ochre c. 1880, diam. 11 cm.

Plate 23   Sowerby's Patent Queen's Ware c. 1878/1879. Small tray in front c. 1878
13 cm diam.

Plate 24   Queen's Ware two-handled dishes c. 1879, 21 cm long, 12.5 cm wide.
Diamond registration mark & Peacock mark.

Plate 26   Mikardo Vase in Queen's ware,
11.5 cm high. Peacock mark.

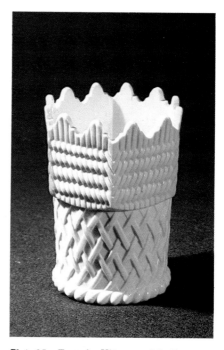

Plate 27   Turquise Vitroporcelain Vase
with basket weave pattern, 10 cm
high.

Plate 30   Swan ornament in Turquoise Vitroporcelain, 16 cm long, 12 cm high,
with trademark.

Plate 31   Sowerby Dolphin bowl, 17 cm diam., 12 cm high (Peacock Trademark):
candlesticks, 5 cm high.

Plate 32   Iridescent Dolphin bowl, 19 cm diam., 11 cm high.

Plate 34   Venetian Series. Jug 22 cm high, Bowl top diam. 12.5 cm

Plate 35   Webb's Iris Glass, 7.5 cm high

Plate 36   Webb's Bronze Glass, 17.5 cm and 12 cm high.

Plate 37   Sowerby Lustre ware. Sugar basin 8.5 cm high, jug 9 cm high.

Plate 38   Sowerby stemmed basin with 'rainbow' iridescence, 11.5 cm high.

Plate 39   Dark lustre Sugar & Cream Set. Basin 12.5 cm high, jug 11 cm high with trademark.

Plate 40   Cranberry Glass. Tallest 8 cm high. Pipe 13.5 cm length.

Plate 43 Butterfly Trinket Set. Tray holding set measures 30 cm long, 22 cm wide.

Plate 44 Watercolour by J.G. Sowerby entitled A Sexton's House, Williamstone, Slaggyford, Carlisle, 28.5 x 34 cm.

Plate 45 Watercolour by J.G. Sowerby entitled The Summons, 21 x 25 cm.

Plate 6   Sowerby Jet Cauldron c. 1880, 6.5 cm high. Peacock trademark.

Plate 7   Cauldron-shaped jet basin (probably Scottish) with thistle pattern mark, and jug. Basin 9 cm high. Jug 7 cm high.

Plate 13   Two blown flint vases with white Peloton decoration, 7 cm high.

Plate 16   Sowerby basket weave patterns c. 1876. Tallest 12.5 cm high all with Peacock mark.

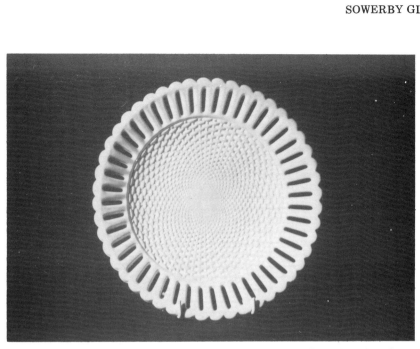

Plate 18   Sowerby White ribbon plate, basket weave pattern. Peacock trademark, 22 cm diam.

Plate 25   Sowerby two handled circular dish, c. 1879, diam. 19.5 cm, flower head pattern on base, diamond registration and Peacock mark.

G

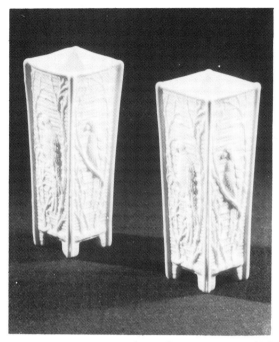

Plate 28   Blanc de Lait glass. Two white slag Parrot vases, 12 cm high. Peacock
mark inside.

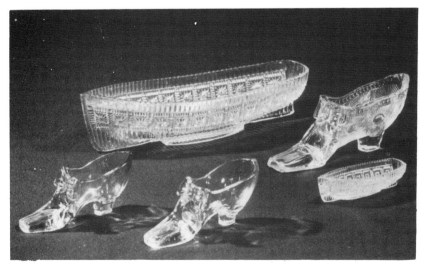

Plate 29   Sowerby Shoe designs and Boats. Largest shoe 21 cm long, 8 cm. high,
large boat 30.5 cm long c. 1895.

Plate 33   Candlestick in Flint glass and small bowl with full Peacock pattern round edge. Jug on right in translucent 'Common' Green; beaker in purple malachite with 'A present from Newcastle' imprinted made for Royal Mining & Industrial Exhibition 1887.

Plate 41   'Tynesyde' Flint Glass Fruit Set. Bowl 15 cm length, 6 fruit dishes 7 cm high.

Plate 42   Sample of Tynesyde Fruit Set in Amber, 5 cm high.

Chapter II

George Davidson & Company

The trade mark of this firm is a demi-lion rising from a turret which has four layers and a scroll underneath and it is easily distinguishable from the lion of the Greener firm which rests on a single scroll. The Davidson lion has been described as a 'demi-lion rampant out of a coronet' [10] but whether the structure is called a coronet or a turret the easily distinguishable difference is the four layered composition against the single scroll. Both lions usually face to the left when present on opaque glass articles but there is obviously a difficulty in deciding which way the lion is facing on a transparent glass article and no reliance for identification can be placed on this at all. (See Introduction, pp.3, 4).

The founder of this firm was George Davidson who was thirty-four years old when he started the glassworks in 1867. He was an Alderman and a Justice of the Peace. Little is known about him personally but his photograph in later life shows him as a bearded gentleman with an honest and open countenance and there was a great family likeness between him and his son Thomas who at the age of 18 started working with him in the firm and continued for thirteen years before succeeding to the firm, in 1891, on the death of George Davidson. When the firm started, paraffin lamps were used for most domestic lighting, and glass chimneys which so greatly improved their efficiency were being imported in quantity from Belgium. George Davidson decided to make chimneys for lamps at the Teams glassworks in Gateshead and he developed a flourishing trade with the so-called Hawkers who slept outside the factory overnight so as to buy the lamp chimneys in the morning as soon as they were cold. Although later, lehrs fired by coal were installed, at that time there were no annealing facilities and the chimneys stood on the floor to become cold overnight. George Davidson augmented his trade by exchanging glass articles made at his works for butter, wheat, tallow, etc., supplied through his brother Joseph who had emigrated to Australia in the mid 19th Century.

Davidson's production stopped completely between January 1880 and May 1881 due to a disastrous fire which, although not damaging the furnaces, destroyed a large part of the warehouses and processing departments. After 1881 more and more domestic tableware products were introduced, the firm made up for lost time and the wide range was very competitive with the products of the other two major firms in the area, Sowerby's and Greener's. Plate 46 shows a vase, pattern No. 107 c. 1885 in transparent blue glass which strangely has a somewhat oily feel.

In the Newcastle Exhibition of 1887 a gold medal was won by the Davidson Company and a Jubilee Plate was produced to commemorate the Jubilee of Queen Victoria. A Davidson Day Book covering 1876 to 1880 shows that the firm had a very wide coverage for sales but their monthly totals did not quite reach the Sowerby levels at this time. Some of the pieces of marble slag glass, black slag and flint glass made by this firm are of very good quality (Plates 47,48). Apart from the trademark it was often difficult to distinguish between similar articles from the three main firms.

61

The Davidson Pearline series however, first registered in 1888 No. 96945 was distinctive. This series was made in transparent canary yellow, a pale but definite blue and a clear glass and all of these articles show a milky appearance on the tops of the articles or on any protrusions (Plate 49). Other attractive Pearline articles have survived the years (see later, p.64).

More is known about Thomas Davidson who took over the running of the firm in 1891 on the death of his father and by that time he was an experienced glassman. Records show that there was no 'blowing' then at the factory which was entirely devoted to pressing. He emerges from the stories as a character, a bachelor but fond of children who was looked after by two old ladies. He lived in a large house in a fashionable private terrace directly overlooking the sea at Tynemouth. The situation of his house near the sea led to him being fined at the beginning of the First World War the sum of ten shillings at North Shields for 'having failed to shade all windows effectively so that no bright light was shed outside'. At 10.5 p.m. on May 16th 1915, the report states, 'a bright light was seen from an attic window. A sergeant got no answer and at 11 o'clock again went to the house. The window was facing the sea and a message had been received from the examination boat complaining about the light. Mr. Davidson said that one of the girls had gone out and left a light burning. He was extremely sorry'.

Tom Davidson worked hard, was inventive, decisive and commanded loyalty and deference, and like his father, he also was a Justice of the Peace. He was a racehorse owner, owning more than a dozen horses at one time and on one of the occasions when Gordon Richards rode his colours he won the Newmarket Stakes on a horse named Wild Son. Tommy Weston, however, was one of the jockeys more favoured by him. He had stables at Richmond in Yorkshire. A newspaper cutting of the time described how Lady Clara, one of his horses was 'remarkably spry out of the slips and goes at a great pace on suitable courses'. The comment continues, 'Mr. Tom Davidson, a northern man, with a voice as big as his body and a heart as big as both gratefully bought her in for 700 guineas'. But Tom Davidson did not like his factory workers to hear him talk of horses.

He was a Director of the Theatre Royal in Newcastle round about 1912 and enjoyed meeting the many famous actors and actresses of the time such as Marie Lloyd, Florrie Ford, Martin Harvey, Dorothy Ward and Tom Walls. The latter was also a racehorse owner and a great friend.

It was a Davidson candlestick, although I did not know this at the time, which started me on the road as a glass collector. The appearance of the metal attracted me and I found later that it was spar glass made at the Davidson Works to a design No. 283 by James Bowran who was head mouldmaker and was aged - unbelievably - 90 years when I last spoke to him. He was coherent, with a reliable memory, active, and an engaging personality. He stated that he must have made over one thousand moulds for the firm from the very small to the really enormous in size. Examples are a one inch mould for a dainty pin tray and a 14" diameter, 20" deep mould for some big street lights which took three months to make and which required six men to press it.

The first mould he attempted was in 1901, when 14 years old. He was then working under Tom Matthews the first Davidson mouldmaker who had returned to England from Germany, where he had been working, to take up the position when the firm started. In this way James Bowran's memories and anecdotes reached back to the early days of this firm. James Bowran later worked under his uncle George Mossman and eventually he himself took charge of the mould shop, clearly a key appointment in any glassworks at that time.

After starting at the Works in 1901 James Bowran became a 'bound' apprentice in 1903 at the age of 16 years which meant that he had a legal obligation to stay with the firm for six years. To use his own words he "had to do the distance or go to court". He remembers Mr. Tom Davidson bringing a group of people which included old Mr. Sowerby to see a mould which he had made when he was nineteen years old and getting the princely sum of two shillings a week. He became a journeyman when twenty-one years old, and stayed with the Davidson firm until his retirement in 1959. He states that Mr. Thomas Davidson was extremely knowledgeable about glass and did the designing of most of the articles himself. I have the impression that there was a comradeship and trust between James Bowran and his employer. He remembered times when he has 'gathered' at the furnace, his uncle has pressed the piece and Mr. Tom Davidson 'a big stout man has worked over the chair'. Thomas Davidson was also intensely interested in colour, spending a lot of his time in the 'mixing' room and he was described as a very thorough man. One of his special colours was Jade, a dense opaque glass, and James Bowran remembers being kept, to the annoyance of his wife, until after midnight one Christmas Eve whilst Mr. Davidson experimented with this colour. Tom Davidson acted swiftly and authoritatively when necessary, for example, in approximately 1913 when James Bowran was about to emigrate to Australia because he thought that the firm were assuming that he 'belonged to them body and soul', a doubling of salary and the gift of a house produced the desired result of keeping him with the firm.

After the First World War under Thomas Davidson, from 1922 onwards, a whole new range of domestic ware was introduced, extra hands were set on, the number of girls and women doubled and the firm flourished. It became a private limited company in 1933, one of the other Directors, with Tom Davidson, being Sir Arthur Lambert, a keen musician and conductor. Thomas Davidson took an active interest in the works until his death in 1937. Indeed his nephew Claude Fraser and James Bowran attended his sick-bed to report progress only two days before he died. In 1937 his nephew became Governing Director, and although Claude L. Fraser did not 'know' glass as his uncle had known it, he was an honest, popular and gentlemanly head of the firm for about twenty years. In 1957 he died while attending a point-to-point race meeting at Corbridge in Northumberland. A short period intervened under the control of Mr. J.M.E. Howarth before the firm became as now the Brama Works under the present owners.

DAVIDSON PATTERNS AND COLOURS

The Rope Pattern vase (Plate 50) in amber glass was made from an early Tom Matthews' mould i.e. in George Davidson's time. The malachite trinket tray with cover (Plate 47) is an example of the colloquially-termed marble slag glass by the Davidson firm, rare because examples of Sowerby's and even Greener's marble slag glass are more common than Davidson's. The example shown is clearly marked with a Davidson lion, and the colour of the marble is rather more brown than the purple of the other two firms. Other marble slag articles e.g. beakers are indistinguishable between the three main firms. Many of the Davidson marble glass articles do not carry a trademark and can be identified only from the Catalogue drawings, such as the purple marble malachite Thimble, about 2" high. This was probably used as a generous measure for spirits, for round the top are the words 'Just a thimbleful' (Plate 47), and it was shown in the catalogue with the Tumblers.

PEARLINE SERIES

The Davidson 'Pearline' series registered in 1888 No. 96945 was attractive, good quality glass. This series was made in transparent canary yellow, a pale but definite blue, a light green and a clear glass, and all of these articles show a milky, pearl-like appearance on the tops or edges of articles. Any raised design or protrusions also show an opal colour in contrast to the translucent body. Articles with this number have a characteristic pattern, (see Plate 49) but other blue pearline articles with different numbers are shown in Plates 51, 52 and 53. Clear glass with an opal-like edge was termed 'Moonshine' which is accurately descriptive for the colour effect is very like moonshine in certain lights (Plate 54). Tom Matthews who had returned from Germany to take up his post kept up his previous connection and occasionally ordered moulds from Germany. Plate 55 shows a yellow pearline boat-shaped vase with an interesting history. It was one of several moulds ordered from Germany being delivered by a ship which became wrecked on the Black Midden rocks at the mouth of the Tyne, as did the ship Crefis recently in 1974, nearly ninety years later. The ship was under water for four years after which some of the moulds were able to be claimed. Some moulds, including different sizes of this pattern, were so corroded at the bottom that George Mossman prepared and substituted new decorated bases. The sides of these moulds are German, bold and clear, while the bases are obviously different with finer detail and closer metal work - clearly the work of two different artisans. James Bowran remembers later melting the Pearline moulds for scrap. Their craftsmanship would be appreciated today.

Yellow Pearline glass (Plate 56) is frequently confused with and mistakenly called Vaseline glass. The latter is completely different being a more delicate yellow colour (with bluish tint), always blown and hand-fashioned, see Plate 57. Pearline in contrast, albeit of an attractive quality is a pressed glass and thus heavier and coarser, and the colour is a harder yellow. The blue coloured Pearline seems to. be the most popular, while the Moonshine and Pale Green colours are the rarest.

BLACK GLASS

The small bowl shown in Plate 58 with a 'satin' finish in black glass was made from a design of 1896. This was a very good selling line so the mould was renewed in the early 1900's and it can still be found in all colours, usually pale blue, pink and amber, sometimes transparent and sometimes acid-finished. Black was the cheapest glass to make but even with this colour it is surprising what a difference there can be depending upon the basic metal and finish. When estimating the amount of Uranium which went into the making of Burmese glass[30], which so pleased Queen Victoria because of its lemon to pink shading, this small black satin bowl (Plate 58) was used as a control. It was approximately the same size as the Burmese glass article, and it was shown not to contain Uranium.

The First World War intervened with its consequent difficulties for all the firms of manpower, supplies and production.

JADE GLASS

As mentioned before one of the special colours which Tom Davidson devised was Jade. This was made in the early nineteen twenties and the Tutankhamun bowl (see p.68) shown in the Frontispiece was made in Jade and black only. Jade coloured glass was continued up to 1928 for the North East Coast Exhibition when the new Tyne Bridge was opened. It is a lovely rich glass often in 'Chippendale' design (see p. 67) and examples are shown in Plates 59 and 60. Felspar was used in its production which gives it a smooth and shiny appearance and made it durable in use. Jade was difficult to deal with in the making because, after five or six hours it used to lose its colour in the pots and if a good colour had been achieved the whole pot would be worked as speedily as possible until empty. Some Jade articles are partly transparent where the colour has begun to disappear. After a few hours if not all used the custom was to 'physic' the glass with five or six potatoes on a long bent steel rod and raise the temperature again to $1500^{\circ}C$. In the last resort black coal dust was added to make use of the mix. Jade articles have special photographic peculiarities. Two articles appearing identical in colour to the naked eye can look a completely different colour, side by side, on the same colour slide (Plate 60).

CLOUD COLOURS

'Cloud' colours started about 1925 and were patented. Although flintglass was rather hard to mix with the cloud colours, black in flintglass produced Purple Cloud. One man gathered a 'moil' from the furnace to make an article and another man with a second 'moil' of a different colour put a small amount on the first. Amber, green and blue cloud colours were made. Black and amber was extremely difficult to make and often used to 'fly', i.e. break, sometimes in front of the workers' eyes when just made, but sometimes as long as two years later, due to different annealing qualities. Cloud colours were melted in a small skittle pot but they could only be made successfully if the two colours were of the same temperature and flexibility. Queen Mary was particularly attracted to blue cloud colour especially if it had been acid finished. Examples are shown in Plate 61. Pure flour and sulphuric acid, made into a light paste, and brushed on to the article produced the 'matt' effect.

Furlux was a flint glass made opaque but this, like Jade, was rather difficult to 'hold' because it gradually went transparent in the pot. James Bowram tells how he had 'truly seen Tom Davidson one day put a bucketful of 'Paris Plaster' in the pot' with an astounding effect which brought out the colour beautifully. His instruction was then to 'work that pot right out in the Furlux'. It went down in the records and although the pot was 'an awful mess' they continued to use Piaster of Paris and he claims that Davidson Furlux was second to none. James Bowran tells of making Paris Plaster models in his office with Tom Davidson beside him 'very enthusiastic and imaginative saying, 'Try this, try that', prior to making the metal moulds.

Royal blue, one of Tom Davidson's last colours and made for the British Industries Fair, was another special colour which once seen can in future be recognised. A handsome large bowl on a deep plinth was made, and one was sent at Queen Mary's request direct to Marlborough House, her residence after the death of King George Vth. In 1937 a Royal Blue Vase won a Diploma of Merit.

Silver sand from Holland was mostly used, but Lochearn sand from Scotland was also rated highly. Knowing this beautiful district in Scotland and the size of the loch such sand cannot have been in very great supply and it would probably be used for special batches. James Bowran was trained to regard iron as the bitter enemy of glass; it 'brought the metal low', i.e. gave it a brownish tinge and even used to eat into and destroy the pots. Because of this two large magnet blades were moved over the silver sand constantly to take the iron out.

Felspar was often used with a smaller amount of lead because the latter was expensive. It made the glass very clear and hard, but although spar was one quarter the cost of lead it made the glass difficult to 'work'.

DAVIDSON MOULDS

Davidson's, once established, made their own moulds. They had a good foundry and their own mixture of cast iron which is thought to be better for moulds than steel, to which glass sometimes adheres. I have had the opportunity of seeing many of James Bowran's old instruments used in the Davidson mould making. For the hammer and chisel work and for the small detail 'diamond' point chisels were used. Depth gauges gave accuracy and a riffler was used to put the finish on the mould after chiselling. A good workman always worked with a warm mould when making it. The smallest mould which James Bowran made was for a glass ball bearing in a scientific instrument. He said that it was the size of an old silver three-penny piece, so small that a lad had to be especially trained to lift out of the furnace only the correct small amount of metal, and the presser had to be 'as quick as grease lightning' to work in time. The biggest mould, although not the heaviest, was a street lighting unit which needed four gatherers to gather it. The heaviest mould, 14½lbs in weight, was for an aeroplane landing light. The glass was made with no lead in it to make it hard so that the wheels of heavy bombers could go over the top of it. If this glass was allowed to flow as it wanted to, James Bowran contended that then the made article could be thrown and it would not break.

I have recently seen a pair of majestic Davidson plain candlesticks in spar glass, at least 1¼ feet tall, of beautiful metal and with James Bowran workmanship patently apparent. They are unblemished and they look as though they would last forever.

Over his career, James Bowran made moulds depicting five different British Sovereigns, i.e. King George V and Queen Mary, Edward VIII, King George VI and Queen Elizabeth II. He used postage stamps as his 'models' but in each case, of course, permission had to be obtained before production commenced. A mould was made also of the head of the Tsar of Russia who was extremely like George V, except for his moustache. It was used to decorate beakers which were made in flint and amber and sent to Russia. These were discontinued, after the assassination of the Tsar. The tankard to celebrate the Coronation of King Edward VIII, which never took place, is unusual (Plate 62). There were also two Davidson glass serviette or napkin rings celebrating the same non-event.

A mould for an ashtray was made depicting the head of one of Tom Davidson's racehorses called 'The President', framed in a horse shoe. I have seen an article from this mould and am told that Tom Walls, the actor, criticised the length of the horse's nose as too long, I think justifiably. Tom Davidson then in fun suggested that the critic should take a hammer and chisel and see how he would fare over such detail.

One mould was made for the four-sided 'Eva' vase with a nude female figure repeated on each panel. It was known colloquially in the Davidson works as the Venus vase. James Bowran posed for me while describing it, with his arms outstretched and uplifted at the elbow to demonstrate to me the figure portrayed, to the astonishment of his gentle wife sitting beside us. She murmured, "I've never heard of that", and he confessed that there was so much 'skit' in the works that he had not ventured to take one home at the time, although an example of every other mould had been taken home - This was a privilege afforded to James Bowran to take one article from each mould that he made. I promised her that if I now found one I would make sure that she saw it even at this belated stage fifty years later. It was made in all colours but not in flint and only in a 10" size. Mr. E. Francis a co-director with Tom Davidson, and head of the London Sale Rooms, more usually concerned with sales, had been responsible for the design.

CHIPPENDALE PATTERN

The Chippendale pattern, see Plates 59 and 60, was used for a great many articles and for a wide range of Davidson table and domestic ware. It was not invented by the Davidson company but the rights and moulds were purchased by them from America, after originating elsewhere in England in George Davidson's time. There is a six-point star on the base of many but not all articles of Chippendale pattern. It was a very successful range and continued for many years until 1959. The examples of jade glass, apart from the Tutankhamun bowl, are of this design.

The Jacobean design, of bevelled squares, was used much later by the Davidson firm in common with a number of other firms, so it is not characteristic.

It had often been not wise to stop James Bowran in the midst of a story for details about persons mentioned because this would lead to a digression and the loss of that particular story. Thus if Mr. Francis is mentioned it is as this name appeared in a story, and a Christian name or other detail is not known.

TUTANKHAMUN BOWL

The fascinating Tutankhamun square bulb bowl (Frontispiece) was made in jade and black only in 1923. It was a Davidson mould made by James Bowran from two drawings given to him by Mr. Francis depicting, he said, a snake charmer and lions and numerous hieroglyphics including a leg, an eye and other symbols. Having been lucky enough to come across one in Jade, I took it poste-haste to James Bowran who before the tissue wrapping was uncovered recognised it saying, "That must be a 'Lions bowl', 1922/23, a Tutankhamun bowl". The mould was made at the time of the original discovery of the Tutankhamun treasures. Although refinements of the Rosetta stone and Egyptology are missing, the pattern is unmistakable and attractive. A great number were made and sold all over Europe but a large proportion of them went to France where enthusiasm for Tutankhamun was greater than here at the time. This probably explains why in this country more have not been seen. This particular bowl demonstrates the difficulty of the jade colour both photographically and in colour 'hold', for in part it is somewhat transparent. I consider this to be a treasure of the time.

James Bowran thinks that the most artistic mould he made was the hobnail basket. This is a hexagonal hobnail in a very refractive pattern and I have seen an example which is very pleasing in amber. He considers that the landing light mould was the most memorable. Thomas Davidson spent much time experimenting and finally perfecting the glass Dome Flower Block which he patented in 1910. It was made in sizes from 2½" up to 10", Patent No. 7830, and it was technically complicated to make. Such technical achievements led to the high regard in which Tom Davidson was held in the trade and to his being elected and holding for many years the office of Chairman of the Glass Manufacturers' Association of the North of England.

On showing James Bowran a covered dense black bowl of Greener design, I wanted his explanation as to why a firm should have decorated so ornately the undersides of articles, where the decoration could not be seen. His first reaction was to clear this point. The mould would also have made for flint glass when the pattern would have been visible through the cover and the underedge of the bowl (See Plate 71). Although the article pleased me as a collector he then commented on it being badly made with a ragged edge because too much glass had been put into the mould, and on what a poor state the mould had been in saying that Thomas Davidson would not have paid his workmen for such work. If he found such articles he might say to the workman, "I'll give it to you to sell and see how you do". An inspection of doubtful articles was undertaken each week by Tom Davidson, James Bowran and a foreman of the glassmakers called Fisher, because the men were on piece work. Tom Davidson was reputedly very fair, meeting the men half way, especially if he realised that a mould or press might have been at fault.

Sowerby's was surely in the lead of coloured pressed glassmaking in the North East of England but it was overtaken by the Davidson firm in the early decades of the 20th Century and the outstanding glass personality of the area in his lifetime was undoubtedly Thomas Davidson. As James Bowran stated, "There was always something exciting or interesting where he was". Whether it was a visit by Martin Harvey when one of the old glassmakers made a large glass hat for him, or a visit by Dorothy Ward and her husband to the glass works or merely 'the old man' standing over him, not interfering but giving useful suggestions or cracking a joke with a hearty laugh, life was interesting and after his death the Davidson world became more humdrum.

Born 1860   Died 1937

Thomas Davidson, Esq., J.P.

Fig. 6

Plate 48   Pair Davidson flint glass salts 7 cm across top, Catalogue No. 96 c. 1885
with Lion mark, and unusual small beaker decorated with windmill,
cottages, etc. with Lion mark, 7.5 cm high.

Plate 46   Davidson blue tulip vase. Pattern no. 207. 22 cm high.

Plate 47   Davidson Marble slag glass. Blue marble glass beaker 11.25 cm high
with Lion trademark. Pin tray with cover (in front) 8.5 cm wide, Lion
trademark on base and on cover. Purple slag glass thimble (for spirit
measure) shown in catalogue with the tumblers. Marble glass salts, on
left Catalogue No. 104 12 cm long; on right Catalogue No. 108. Marble
glass vase Catalogue No. 237, 10.5 cm high.

H

Plate 49   Davidson Pearline Series 1888 R^D 96945. 2 dishes and 2 beakers in Blue
Pearline, largest 28 cm wide. Small yellow pearline vase 9 cm high, and
Moonshine Pearline basket 16.5 cm long.

Plate 50   Rope pattern vase 9 cm high.

Plate 51   Blue Pearline basin and jug R.D 130643.
Basin 11 cm high, jug 10 cm high

Plate 52   Blue Pearline Series. Basket with handle R.D 130643, 17 cm. diam.
Basin 11.5 cm diam. and 2 small ornaments 5 cm high.

Plate 53   Blue Pearline Series Basket R.D 160241 (1890) 17 cm long axis and
blue hobnail pattern vase.

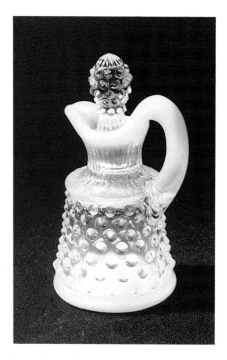

Plate 54   Moonshine toilet bottle 12 cm high (matching candlesticks with dome base were made in this pattern).

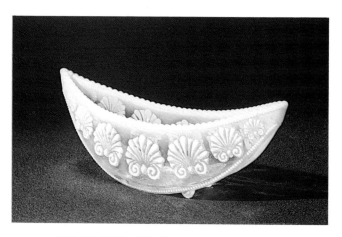

Plate 55   Yellow Pearline boat, 23.5 cm long axis.

Plate 56   Yellow Pearline articles. Square vase 8.5 cm high, larger vase 15 cm high, small vase with handles 8.5 cm high.

Plate 57   Vaseline glass 7 cm high, 13 cm across top.

Plate 59   Jade Trinket set. Tray holding toilet articles and candlesticks 33 cm long 20 cm wide.

Plate 5 8   Black 'satin' glass bowl Davidsons 1 0 cm diam. 7 cm high and shiny
black vase with Davidson trademark.

Plate 6 0   Davidson Jade Vases. Chippendàle pattern.

Plate 6 1   Davidson's Cloud Colours. Blue & Amber vases 1 4 cm high, Purple vase
19 cm high. Small purple bowl 1 2 cm across, Blue bowl, often in dark
blue and other colours and often on black glass stand.

Frontispiece. Davidson's Tutankhamun bowl. Jade Glass. 1923.
15.5 cm square, 8 cm high.

Fig. 7 . Mr. & Mrs. James Bowran.
Mr. Bowran made the mould for the above piece.

Plate 62   King Edward VIIIth Commemorative tankard, 1 0 .5 cm high. Bears
legend 'Long live the King, Crowned 1 9 3 7 '.

Chapter III

Greener & Company

Less is known about the personalities and operations of the Greener Company in its early days. According to L.M.A. Butterworth, Robert Greener who was an expert in glass cutting first had premises in High Street, Sunderland [36] and he and his family started the firm of Angus & Greener when taking over the Wear Flint Glass Works in Sunderland. I.W.S. of Barking, Essex, however in a letter published in a Sowerby scrapbook stated that Henry Greener who worked at the Sowerby firm in Gateshead left there in 1857, to start pressed glass making in Sunderland with James Angus at the Wear Flint Glass Works in 1858. However the Angus & Greener firm started, H. Greener registered a demi-lion holding a star and with a scroll at the base, as a trademark in 1878. (See Introduction p.4). It is probable that Henry Greener joined the family flint glass firm to start pressed glass work.

It is not surprising that there are similarities between the products of the North East firms making pressed glass in the late 19th Century because there was interchange of work people and Henry Greener himself must have taken much Sowerby expertise to his firm.

In 1871 Henry Greener became head of the business and bought some land where James A. Jobling & Co. now stands. In 1885 the Wear Flint Glass Works were in financial trouble and were taken over by James Augustus Jobling who was a chemical merchant in Newcastle upon Tyne. He had supplied the Greener firm with most of its chemicals for coloured glass, and he was owed a great deal of money by the firm. At that time, a great number of articles were being produced by the Greener firm, and Henry Greener renewed the registration of the lion trademark on 17th December 1890.

Some surviving examples of Greener glass are of rather poor quality yet they always have a certain appeal of design which is characteristic, but others were expertly finished and produced.

Early in the 20th Century James A. Jobling was joined by his nephew Ernest Jobling Purser and the latter expanded the firm producing many coloured glass products. He eventually secured a licence and the sole rights to manufacture 'Pyrex' in this country for England and the overseas Dominions. Pyrex was a heat resistant glass ware from the Corning Glass Works in the U.S.A., and the first Pyrex products were produced in Sunderland in 1921. This transparent oven ware had novel attractiveness at the time when compared to the old-fashioned brown ware. Adam Dodds, the manager of the rival Sowerby firm had visited the Corning Glassworks in America in October 1920. His comment about the visit read, 'The Corning Glass Works make beautiful fancy goods also the Pyrex Cooking Ware. I spent a whole day to visit these works expecting to see this wonderful Pyrex glass made or hoped so at any rate but the Dr in charge, the head chemist of 25, conducted the party and never allowed any out of his sight and kindly showed us how to make bulbs &c by machinery.' Mr. Dodds had a sarcastic turn of phrase sometimes in his reports.

The firm produces today a wide range of glass for scientific purposes (employing skilled glass blowers) but mainly, still manufactures the famed oven glass ware 'Pyrex'. Thus there is not competition today between the three firms, Sowerby's (Suntex) being engaged in producing toughened car windscreens and what is best described as anti-bandit glass, Joblings in specialised ovenware, and the old Davidson firm in metal and glass table ware.

In the late 19th Century, however, competition was fierce and each of the firms seemed to know the other's prices, credits and difficulties and took account of these. In spite of the lack of anecdote and legend the Greener pieces of glass from the 19th and early 20th century still to be found are full of fascination, and the surviving glass tells its own tale.

TRADEMARK

All the pieces shown in the plates are genuinely Greener pieces with the lion trademark. This mark is sometimes stated to be a lion with an axe. As explained previously when the lion is holding an implement it is more properly described as a halberd being a combination of axe and spear, but only about a quarter of the 'marked' articles have this implement. When present it is usually very prominent. About three-quarters of the articles marked with the lion do not exhibit a halberd and some of these marks are extremely defined and visible. It is a calculated omission of the implement rather than an inexact casting of the trademark, and close inspection shows the lion to be holding a star as in the Registration shown below. This appeared in Trade & Industry, Journal No. 96 dated 1877.

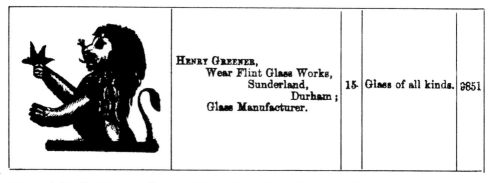

	Henry Greener, Wear Flint Glass Works, Sunderland, Durham ; Glass Manufacturer.	15.	Glass of all kinds.	9851

It is probable that because the star did not show distinctly and well this lion was confused with the lion used by the Davidson firm at the same time and the halberd could have been added to overcome this difficulty and thus is found on the later Greener goods i.e. about mid-1880's onwards.

GREENER PATTERNS

Plate 63 shows a sweetmeat dish. An amethyst and an amber jug are also shown with an attractive style, the handle being placed fairly low - The marks show no halberd - Neither does the Greener flint dish on a stand (Plate 64), the lion holds a star (as above). This small article is refractive and has much detail on the pressed stem making it appear as a creditable imitation of cutting. This was a feature of early pressed glass everywhere, but eventually pressed glass became popular and the manufacturers began to exploit the advantages of pressing and moulding and gradually ceased to emulate the detail of hand made cut glass. The early pressed pieces such as that shown in the Plate 64 are thus interesting and unusual, the stem here emulating a faceted cut stem. The diamond registration mark dated it as 1882. The flint plate also shown with open edges and rose

Round, 5, 6, 7½, 9, 11¼ Inch.

pattern is similarly intricate and moulded. The lion on this article holds a star (as above).

Even up to 1886 certain pressed articles had the feel of cut glass, for example see Plate 65 and drawing. This bowl with the Sowerby peacock trade mark and registered number of 44659 of 1886 has the refractive appeal of the early pressed glass and sharp moulding on the outside of the article.

A hitchy-dobber carrying a moulded image of Queen Victoria and dated 1837-1897 is shown in Plate 66. This relic of the childhood game of hopscotch where the 'dobber' was hitched along with the foot from one bay to another shows many signs of wear and play. Such articles were made frequently by the workmen, out of bottle glass, and taken home for their children. This portrait of the Queen has been ascribed to the Greener firm.

MALACHITE AND OTHER SLAG GLASS

Sometimes the malachite purple marbled ware of the Greener firm varies from that produced by the other two firms being of a paler purple colour and with less white marbling (Plate 67) but other articles are almost indistinguishable, except for the trademarks. The mark on the Greener marble beaker in Plate 68 is very clear, the lion facing left and holding a halberd.

Greener's early purple malachite was sometimes rather bluish in colour, for example the 'Salt' shown in Plate 68. In contrast the 'crinoline' lady shown in Plate 3 is in marble ware which is of typical American colour and style. There is probably more variation in the colour of Greener's purple marble ware articles than in those of the other two firms.

A Greener white slag basin (Plate 69) with rose and thistle pattern is well made and of good quality, as is also, the blue slag plate with a grape and vine pattern and open latticed edge (see Frontispiece). The contrast with the Sowerby basket weave plate is evident (see Plate 17). There are far fewer Greener plates available than Sowerby plates. Neither are found easily but the Greener plate is almost a rarity.

COMMEMORATIVE VASE

An extremely rare pale green marble goblet-shaped vase marked with the Greener lion holding a star is shown in Plate 70. It is a commemorative vase depicting Princess Louise, Duchess of Argyll and her husband the Marquis of Lorne. Princess Louise was the fourth daughter of Queen Victoria but she was the first daughter to marry a commoner and the first to remain in England after her wedding, which took place in St. George's Chapel, Windsor on 21st March 1871 [37] . Both of these facts caught the public interest and imagination, which was augmented because of her artistic talents which were exceptional in sculpture and in painting, both in watercolour and in oils, and because she did not easily conform to court discipline. They were a popular couple and when he became Governor General of Canada for five years this Greener design commemorated the event and their departure from England in November 1878. While in Canada, Princess Louise fostered art schools and art galleries and continued her own work. When opening the Montreal Gallery she gave one of her own pictures and she also gave a large oil painting to the National Gallery of Ottawa, as well as a portrait she had made of Miss Clara Montalba, the artist. The commemorative article shown in Plate 70 is of very high quality, well-produced and designed and it can be classed as a Museum piece.

JET GLASS

Some of the Greener articles, as already stated, are of poorer finish although it seems to be a question of poor quality control rather than poor quality of design or of the metal. A jet covered basin for example (Plate 71) is of good design and quality but too much metal has been in the mould and the edges of the lid are uneven - the pattern and glass however are good. It might be wondered why a firm would decorate so elaborately the underside of the cover and the underside edge of a butter dish. The reason is that this mould would also have been used for flint, i.e. colourless glass when the pattern would show through and be decorative. This point should often be remembered. For example many purple malachite wares with their swirling colours have elaborate pressed decoration which seems at first to be typically Victorian overindulgence. The simple explanation is that the moulds were really made to cater for flint wares which were far more common at that time than coloured wares. The black dish is marked very clearly on both dish and cover with the Greener lion with a halberd.

The vivid blue transparent beaker (Plate 72) is another example of good quality Greener glass - good design but poor production, because the mould marks are very clearly visible and the edge of the beaker is deficient and ragged. It has a pattern on the outside in imitation of cutting.

The shiny jet black dish (Plate 73) Registered No. 777133 has a typical Jobling grape cluster pattern - and a similar pattern but different shape was registered a year later and can be found in a shiny rather oily looking green colour.

JOBLING'S OPALIQUE

When Ernest Jobling Purser took over at the Greener firm there was a period of about ten years, approximately 1910 to 1920, when the firm worked under the name of Jobling's, producing table ware and decorative glass. At that time René Lalique in France had become very well known as a glass artist and in particular his opalescent type glass was in demand. Jobling's for a very short time produced a similar type of glass, which they called Opalique, some being of very good design and quality. For example, Plate 74 shows a pair of Art Nouveau style candlesticks with very good finish and with an engraved marking on the base 'Jobling's Opalique'. The flower in the pattern forms the holder for the candle, the workmanship of the mould is excellent and the articles are made from heavy good quality glass. The small model of a fish on a stand (Plate 75) is of similar quality, and is an early example of Opalique. The name 'Opalique' and 'Patent applied for' is engraved on the base. The plate (Plate 76) with a pattern of three birds is in the same type of glass, but not quite such good quality. It is of a later date marked Opalique No. 780217. This bird pattern was produced also in the shape of a bowl (compare Plate 11).

The Beamish Museum at Stanley, Co. Durham, owns three lovely pieces of Jobling's Opalique; one is a fish model much larger than the one shown in Plate 75 Registered No. 799629; one is an elephant, with trunk outstretched, Registered No. 795793, and the last piece depicts two Lovebirds Registered No. 788543, about four inches high, the quality of which would vie with Lalique glass in any setting. These three articles were made about 1933/34 and were probably the last examples made. The small output of 'Opalique' glass and its quality make it sought after by collectors.

After 1921 James A. Jobling & Co., became fully committed to the specialised ovenware, Pyrex, and have progressed and expanded along this line ever since.

Their output of ornamental and coloured articles during the turn of the Century was less than either Sowerby's or Davidson's, and surviving articles by this firm are therefore rather rare.

I

Plate 6 3   Greener's sweetmeat dish, amber and amethyst jugs. Lion holding
a Star trademark.

Plate 6 7   Greener marbled vase, 2 2 cm high. Lion trademark holds star.

Plate 68   Greener marble slag ware. Beaker 12 cm high. Lion holding halberd.
Vase 13.5 cm high, Lion holding star. 'Salt' 9.5 cm long, Lion holding
star.

Plate 72   Greener blue beaker with handle
Lion holding star trademark

Plate 74   'Jobling's Opalique' candlesticks, incised mark on base, 12 cm high,
7 cm diam. base.

Plate 75   Opalique Fish ornament, 8 cm long, 5 cm high. 'Opalique' 'Patent
applied for' on base.

Plate 76   Opalique plate No. 780217 diam. 26 cm.

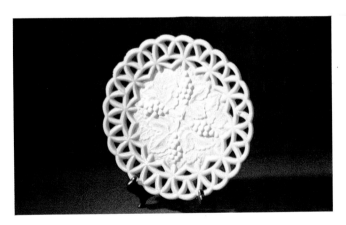

Frontispiece   Turquoise plate by Greener. Grape & Vine pattern,
                latticed edge, 22.5 cm diam. Trademark, Lion with star.

Plate 64   Greener flint dish with faceted stem, 10 cm high c. 1882 and Greener lace edged plate, diam 22 cm. Lion holding a star on each item.

Plate 65   Sowerby flint bowl 1886 refractive No. 44659, 29.5 cm diam.

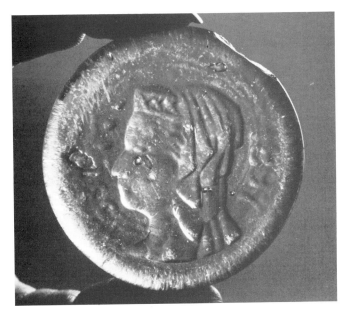

Plate 66   Hitchy-dobber (Greener)

Plate 69   Greener white slag basin, 14 cm high. Lion holding star.

Plate 70   Greener pale green marbled Com-
            memorative goblet, 11 cm high
            1878. Lion trademark clearly
            holding a star (see p 74).

Fig. 8   Watercolour by Princess Louise

Plate 71 Greener Jet slag basin and cover 13.5 cm diam. Both basin and cover show Lion trademark with halberd.

Plate 73 Jet bowl. Greener Rd 777133, 21.5 cm diam.

Chapter IV

Pressed Glass of other North East Firms

Although some other North-east firms did not have trade marks which identify their goods, patents or registration numbers allow identification of some interesting patterns.

W. H. HEPPLE & CO.

W.H. Hepple & Co. of Newcastle upon Tyne patented a miniature coal-truck as used in the mines, in 1880. I have seen it in various sizes, both in flint and in blue transparent glass. This firm also registered a fish jug in 1882 with a detailed pattern of fish scales (Plate 77). This example is in a good purple malachite slag glass but it was produced also in white slag glass and other colours. A matching sugar basin with the same pattern of fish scales is seen in Plate 77. W.H. Hepple & Co. also produced ornaments of pressed glass lions to commemorate the placing of the Landseer lions at the base of Nelson's Monument in Trafalgar Square. They can be found occasionally and are of various sizes and in different colours. But other firms produced these also and it is not possible to say accurately which firm was responsible for the heavy pressed glass vase in black (Plate 78) with three lions forming the feet of the vase. This vase was also made in alabaster glass. The articles of the W.H. Hepple & Co. firm are all of good quality and production.

EDWARD MOORE & CO.

Edward Moore & Co. at the Tyne Flint Glassworks were established in Holborn, South Shields in 1861 — Certainly a bottle was registered by this firm on June 20th of that year. Edward Moore worked for some years at the Sowerby firm in Gateshead before starting on his own in South Shields. He was reputed to be 'courteous, hard-working and a real gentleman'. The firm produced an attractive eight-sided 'hob-nail' pattern which resembled cut glass. It was made in good amber colour in basket designs, jugs, etc.

Because of the firm's difficulties in 1913, many of the firm's moulds and presses were sold by auction. Adam Dodds of Sowerby's Ellison Glassworks bought many of the articles at reasonable prices, but the pick of the moulds he stated went privately to the Davidson firm. Edward Moore & Co. eventually liquidated voluntarily in 1922.

JAMES HARTLEY OF WEAR GLASS WORKS

James Hartley of Wear Glass Works was an old established firm in Sunderland which made glass for the Crystal Palace in 1851 and later became famous for its coloured glass [38] — One of their patterns of the late 19th Century is shown in Plate 79. The pattern on the pair of plates in amber glass is very refractive, and the words 'Give us this day our Daily Bread' form the border decoration. It is an example of good mould work, good production and good metal. Whether the 'Present for a good boy' small plate, also shown, delighted its young recipient or not is guesswork. Perhaps it did.

MATTHEW TURNBULL OF THE CORNHILL GLASSWORKS

Matthew Turnbull of the Cornhill Glassworks in Sunderland made another fairly well known plate pattern. This is the crossed swords pattern celebrating the Golden Jubilee of Queen Victoria in 1887 (Plate 80) as distinct from the 60 years reign celebrations of 1897. The plate shown is in a bright translucent blue but was also made in amber and other colours. This firm liquidated in 1954.

THE TYNE PLATE GLASS COMPANY

The Tyne Plate Glass Company in 1850 was probably responsible for production of the glass 'book' shown in Plate 81; Such would be used in pairs as book ends or separately for ornaments. The example shown is a beautifully clear pale green pure metal and nicely hand cut - the workmanship is very good. Similar articles were produced in black glass and an example can be seen in the South Shields Museum.

Plate 79   Amber bread plates, 24 cm diam. 'Give us this day our Daily Bread' forms border decoration (James Hartley). Small plate 'A present for a good boy', diam. 12.5 cm.

Plate 81   Book ornament, handcut. 17.5 cm long x 12.5 cm wide.

Chapter V

Coloured Blown Glass of the North East;
Mid 19th. Century

MID 19th CENTURY AND EARLIER

GIMMEL FLASKS, etc.

The gimmel flask shown in Plate 82 is engraved with a picture of the High Level Bridge in Newcastle on one side and the words 'Matthew Batty 16th June 1882' on the other side. These double flasks with necks pointing in the opposite direction were made as early as 1660 to contain oil and vinegar. One fluid could be poured without spilling the other, and corks were used for closures. This particular flask has an almost invisible thin sheet of glass dividing the two flasks. Its presence can be confirmed only by filling one side with liquid or by inserting a needle attached to a thread through one of the necks. The needle is then seen to rest on the transparent dividing glass. The High Level Bridge between Gateshead and Newcastle is a two-tier structure. The upper bridge carrying railway lines was opened by Queen Victoria in 1849 but the lower road bridge was not completed and opened until 1850.

Some of these flasks were made in flint or opaque white glass with decoration of coloured loops in the glass. This type of decorated glass is now frequently but mistakenly called Nailsea Glass. Although it was made at Nailsea many other glassworks including Sunderland and Newcastle produced similar articles. Plate 83 shows a decanter of flint glass with white loops, also a flask similarly fashioned and a decorative ornamental pipe.

ROLLING PINS

Rolling pins were often bought as presents by sailors for their wives and sweethearts. Some were hung in the house superstitiously to bring good luck, others were functional and used to contain salt, the pins being suspended from the chimney piece to keep the salt dry. Most were probably in the first category. Plate 84 shows the only small child's rolling pin which I have seen. It is 8¼" long compared to the usual 15" or 16", is decorated with the words 'For a good girl 1855', and was obviously made for a favoured child relative. In the same category of goods were the flasks in the shape of bellows, or musical instruments, and walking sticks or shepherd's crooks made of glass. All over the counrty such 'friggers' or 'whimsies' were common. The sturdy walking stick in Plate 85 is a north country example and made from good heavy green glass with a twisted black glass thread running ghrough it.

OPALINE and 'BRISTOL' BLUE

The white opaline glass sugar basin and creamer Plate 86 is of earlier origin, probably late 18th Century or very early 19th Century. The glass has a fiery appearance when held up to the light. The foot has a turned-over edge and a fairly high 'kick' in the dome of the foot, showing the pontil mark where the glass was held during fashioning. The cream jug and the fashioning of the handle with its looped application and turned-over end helps to date this pair. They are decorated in north country style. A similar basin although probably a little later, is shown in Plate 87 decorated with the words 'Be canny with the sugar' - canny being a north country and Scottish word meaning 'careful'. This basin is in a lovely blue colour often mistakenly called Bristol Blue. Although Bristol Blue is famous, similar coloured glass was made in other localities and this north country example on a stem and foot has a simple north country style of flower decoration which is still in excellent condition. Because this type of decoration was not fired into the glass, on most examples of such articles the decoration is in poor condition or has been completely removed with washing and wear. This one must have been treasured over the years to have remained in such pristine condition. I have seen exactly the same article, where the decoration had worn off with time, put up for sale as a Georgian Goblet.

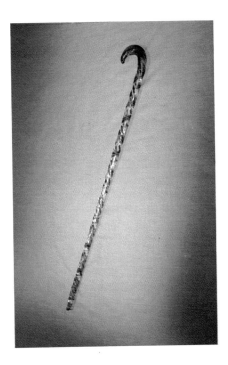

Plate 85   Walking Stick 80 cm long. Twisted black glass thread running through green glass.

Plate 87   Blue basin decorated with words 'Be Canny with the Sugar', 13.5 cm high.

Plate 77   Fish jug and basin. W.H. Hepple & Co. Basin 14 cm diam. jug 17.5 cm high.

Plate 78   Jet glass vase, 19 cm high.

Plate 80 'Crossed Swords' Plate 20.5 cm diam. (Matthew Turnbull).

Plate 82 Engraved Gimmel Flask. June 1882 24 cm long

Plate 83   Flask, pipe and decanter with looped white decoration.

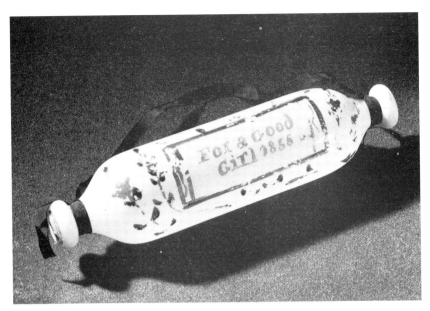

Plate 84   Child's Rolling Pin, 20.5 cm long decorated with words 'For a Good Girl 1855'.

Plate 86   Opaline sugar basin and cream. Basin 11 cm diam., cream 12 cm high.

References

1. McKenzie, E., and Dent, History of Northumberland, Vol. 1, pp 208-212, St. Nicholas' Church Yard 1811.

2. Local Directories of 1800—1834, Vols. 4 and 5 of Gateshead and Newcastle upon Tyne, compiled from local newspapers. Gateshead Public Library, Archives and Local History Department.

3. 13th Report of the Commissioners of Excise Enquiry, 1835, Appendix No. 7.

4. Manders, F.W.D., A History of Gateshead, 1973, Gateshead Council.

5. Sykes, John, Local Records or Historical Register of Remarkable Events, T. & J. Hodgson, Newcastle 1823, pp 344—345.

6. The Victoria History of the Counties of England. Durham Vol. 11, 1907. Reprinted by Davisons, London, 1968.

7. Rewcastle, J., A record of the Great Fire in Newcastle and Gateshead, to which is prefixed a History of Newcastle, 1855. George Routledge & Co., London.

8. An Account of the Great Fire and Explosion which occurred in Newcastle on Tyne and Gateshead on 6th October 1854, pp 17; 51—77. H. & M.W. Lambert, Hunter & Co., Newcastle, and A. Hall, Virtue & Co., London.

9. Walton, Clarence R., The Town's Oldest Industry — Glassmaking, Gateshead. Memories and Portraits, Northumberland Press Ltd., Gateshead on Tyne, 1940.

10. Ridley, Ursula, The History of Glass Making on Tyneside, Circle of Glass Collectors, No. 122, January 1961.

11. Pilbin, Preston, Journal of the Tyneside Geographical Society of Newcastle upon Tyne. No. 1, October 1936, New Series Vol. 1, pp 31—45.

12. Clephan, James, Pamphlets 1875-1880   3. The Manufacture of Glass in England. The Rise of the Art on the Tyne, 1879. Reprinted from Archaeologia Aeliana of the Society of the Antiquaries of Newcastle upon Tyne, 1879.

13. Gros-Galliner, Gabriella, Collector's Extravaganza or Beilby Enamelled Glass, Collectors Guide, September 1970.

14. Rush, James, The Ingenious Beilbys, Barrie & Jenkins, London 1973.

15. Historic Architecture of Newcastle upon Tyne, Oriel Press 1967. Edited by Bruce Allsopp.

16. Hall, Marshall, The Artists of Northumbria, p 62, 1973. Marshall Hall Associates, Newcastle upon Tyne.

17. Sowerby, J.G., Rooks and Their Neighbours, 1895. Mawson, Swan & Morgan, Newcastle upon Tyne. Gay & Bird, London.

18. Houfe, Simon, Dictionary of Book Illustrators & Caricaturists 1800–1914., 1978 Antique Collectors Club.

19. Amaya, Mario, Art Nouveau, Studio Vista Ltd. 1866, London

20. Madsen, S. Tschudi, Art Nouveau, World University Library, London, 1967.

21. Trade & Industry, Vol. 23, 30th April 1976.

22. The Pottery Gazette, January 1, 1880.

23. McClinton, Katherine Morrison, Lalique for Collectors 1975 pp 2, 48. Lutterworth Press, Guildford and London.

24. Garner, Philippe, 'Emile Gallé', 1976 p 99. Academy Editions, London.

25. 'The Tyneside', Newcastle and District. An Epitome of Results and Manual of Commerce, 1889. Historical Publishing Co., Newcastle, London, Edinburgh and Leeds.

26. Revi, A.C., (Revised Edition) Nineteenth Century Glass, Its Genesis and Development. 1967 pp 245–263. Thomas Nelson & Sons, London.

27. Gros-Galliner, Gabriella, Glass, A Guide for Collectors. Frederick Muller Ltd., London. 1970.

28. Willis, Geoffrey, English and Irish Glass 1968, Victorian Glass Part 2. 15. p 2 Guiness Signatures, London.

29. Godden, Geoffrey A., Antique China and Glass under £5. Arthur Barker Limited, London. 1966.

30. Murray, S.M. and Haggith, J.W., Radioactive Beauty of Burmese Glass, Collectors Guide, pp 85–86 October 1970.

31. Murray, S.M. and Haggith, J.W., Chameleon-Like Uranium Glass and How to Identify It, The Antique Collector pp 215-218 October/November 1971.

32. Murray, S.M., and Haggith, J.W., The Estimation of Uranium in Colored Glasses, Journal of Glass Studies, Volume XV pp 184-186 1973, The Corning Museum of Glass, New York, U.S.A.

33. Morris, Barbara, Victorian Table Glass and Ornaments. 1978. Barrie & Jenkins, London.

34. Lattimore, Colin R., English 19th Century Press-moulded Glass. 1979. Barrie & Jenkins, London.

35. Pellatt, Apsley, Curiosities of Glassmaking. 1849. D. Bogue, London.

36. Butterworth, L.M. Angus, British Table & Ornamental Glass. 1956. pp 63—64. J.W. Arrowsmith Ltd., Bristol.

37. Duff, David, The Life Story of H.R.H. Princess Louise, Duchess of Argyll. 1940 Stanley Paul & Co. Ltd., London.

38. Bowling, H.C., Coombs, L.C., and Walton, R., The land of the Three Rivers, The Tyne, The Wear and The Tees. 1958. McMillan & Co. Ltd., London.

Index